*Recognizing Other Subjects*

# Recognizing Other Subjects

Feminist Pastoral Theology
and the Challenge of Identity

## Katharine E. Lassiter

PICKWICK *Publications* · Eugene, Oregon

RECOGNIZING OTHER SUBJECTS
Feminist Pastoral Theology and the Challenge of Identity

Pickwick Publications
An Imprint of Wipf and Stock Publishers
199 W. 8th Ave., Suite 3
Eugene, OR 97401

www.wipfandstock.com

ISBN: 978-1-4982-3037-7

*Cataloging-in-Publication data:*

Lassiter, Katharine E.

Recognizing other subjects : feminist pastoral theology and the challenge of identity / Katharine E. Lassiter.

xii + 188 p.; 23 cm—Includes bibliographical references and index.

ISBN: 978-1-4982-3037-7

1. Pastoral theology. 2. Feminist theology 3. Theology, practical. I. Title.

BV4011 L38 2015

Manufactured in the USA

*Para mi Camilita*

# Contents

# Acknowledgments

This project was never mine alone. I encountered many along the way who have shaped this project and have shaped me. I recognize, acknowledge, and am grateful for everyone's generosity.

This work began during graduate school at Vanderbilt University and I am thankful for the all the opportunities I was offered to think about subjectivity, social justice, and suffering. I am deeply grateful for my dissertation advisor, Bonnie Miller-McLemore, who modeled generous and generative support. Thank you for inviting me to become a colleague in the enterprise of feminist pastoral theology and for creating space for me in the Religion, Psychology, and Culture program. Additional thanks go to my committee members, Barbara McClure, Ellen Armour, and Jaya Kasibhlata for engagement with my project, and for their continued engagement with me as I grow as a scholar and teacher. I am also thankful for the funding, support, and innovative pedagogy I experienced as a Theology and Practice Fellow from 2006–2012. That generous financial support continued with a dissertation publication assistance grant, with thanks to Jaco Hamman. Thank you Ted Smith, Jin Young Choi, Angela Cowser, Sean Hayden, and Asante Todd for sharing deep, mutual formation with me. I am especially grateful to fellow Theology and Practice alumna Natalie Wigg-Stevenson who invited me to think about the nature of desire. Thank you to Andrea Tucker who gently pushed me to read unfamiliar critical theory with her. I am also grateful for the academic mentorship I experienced as part of the Global Feminisms Collaborative from 2009–2011, a group of junior and senior feminist scholars who nurtured my questions. I also extend deep thanks to Robin Jensen and Patout Burns who opened their mountain view home for connections and merriment.

Thank you to the Institute of Pastoral Studies at Loyola University Chicago for inviting me to serve as a Lilly extern during academic year 2011–2012. Heidi Russell deserves a huge reward on this earth for sharing her quiet office space with big windows with me. Thank you Susan Rans, Bob Ludwig, Diane Maloney, Steve Krupa, Eileen Daily, Mary Froehle, and especially Bob O'Gorman for encouraging me during that year and in the years since. I remain deeply grateful for the students who enrolled in the courses Foundations of Social Justice, Diversity and Equity, and Listening Skills for Social Justice Practitioners. Our conversations to define and enact justice in light of difference at interpersonal, social-political, and theological levels made me a better writer and teacher and are reflected in this manuscript.

I am grateful for the continued support of my research and the opportunities to engage my faculty colleagues at Mount St. Joseph University. Many thanks go to Jennifer Morris and Elizabeth Mason for sharing a chipper attitude and encouraging my writing. John Trokan, my department chair, encouraged this work in many ways, but especially through a very practical teaching schedule. I am thankful that Marge Kloos invited me to teach about particular experiences of social injustice as we launched a new core curriculum, allowing my research to inform my teaching and vice versa. Continued thanks also goes to the Dean of Arts & Humanities, Mike Sontag, who graciously invites me to ask questions and give responses that draw from my research and teaching. It bears saying that this manuscript, which began as a dissertation, has undergone significant revision, hopefully for the better, in conversation with my colleagues and while teaching undergraduate and Master's students. While pastoral research initially shaped the dissertation project, and still continues to shape this form of it, I would be remiss if I failed to acknowledge my gratitude for the undergraduate and graduate students I have taught over the past three years, particularly students enrolled in Personal Spirituality and Theology of Human Experience, Disabling Theology, and Critical Issues in Sexuality & Spirituality. Thank you all for your willingness to dive deep, forcing me to encounter my own assumptions and privilege.

Very special thanks go to those individuals who have allowed me to share parts of their stories, especially those whose names appear in this text as Stephen, Sarah, and Fr. Gene. I am grateful to many more, especially Annie Hardison-Moody and Mindy McGarrah Sharp, my writing partners and dear friends, who encourage my writing, hold me accountable, and sharpen my thought. I am thankful for the intellectual and emotional support and challenge of family and friends: Tim Fluhr, Alesandra Bellos, Sarah Bellos, Katy Hansen, my brother Charlie, and my parents Paula and Clinton. I am especially grateful for the ongoing gift of friendship with Jen Hale. Last, a special note of thanks to my sister Clare Lassiter for her support and willingness to allow me to accompany her and Camila as part of my journey toward flourishing.

To all those who may see themselves in these pages, but who I may have overlooked, or chosen not to name as we know that this is a serious game: thank you. Our project of co-becoming as selves-in-relation continues.

# Introduction

How do we become ourselves? What role do primary caregivers, social and political institutions, and religious communities play in shaping our becoming? What happens when our becoming conflicts with the ideal desires and norms of the people and institutions in which we live and move and have our being? What happens when our selves are formed in material and relational poverty? How do we begin to speak of these questions from a pastoral theological viewpoint? How do we enact a pastoral praxis that does justice while caring? These large and layered questions guide the development of my thought on the challenges of identity in constructing a feminist pastoral theology of subjectivity.

After twenty years of significant contribution—directly addressing issues from and for women in pastoral theologies of care—the field of feminist pastoral theology has not adequately reflected on the construction of its female subject and the role of identity in this task. The field has primarily offered pastoral theologies of care based on an identity framework. An identity framework, whether of single identity such as "women" or of intersecting identities such as "black women" or "lesbian women," is problematic. First, identity alone cannot capture the full complexity of subjectivity. Second, identity can be used to disable the ability of a subject to give an account of herself. My goal in writing is to reflect on the challenges of identity in constructing theological anthropologies. I do so by examining theories of recognition drawn from psychoanalytic theory, social theory, and theology, and putting them into conversation with feminist pastoral theology.

## Motherhood, Revisited

This particular project began to take shape as I reflected on my commitment to bring a social justice lens to the discipline and practice of feminist pastoral theology. As a community-engaged feminist pastoral theologian and researcher, I believe that good theory is born from reflecting on the human condition in all its possibilities and limitations. Likewise pastoral practice demands engagement with theories and theologies in which challenges to care are identified. As such, I pay attention to material conditions and to the body to develop a feminist pastoral theology of recognition. In paying attention to the body and material conditions we ensure that the care of the soul is not rendered body-less. I understand this as a grounded pastoral theology which engages the complexity of human subjectivity. While lived experience and practical wisdom undergird this project, I also use interdisciplinary resources to reflect on human experience. I draw from psychoanalysis, critical social theory, and liberation theology to describe the limits of an identity framework in feminist pastoral theology. I argue that framing questions of subject formation in light of theories of recognition provides new avenues for conceptual and practical work in feminist pastoral theology.

Motherhood is one particular location where I encountered questions of social justice and subjectivity in feminist pastoral theology. My intellectual engagement on motherhood happened when I met Stephen. Stephen was an Episcopalian minister-theologian who described a central dilemma he faced while serving as a hospital chaplain. He narrated that a woman had given birth to a non-viable fetus at full-term. She asked for her daughter to be named and baptized in the Christian tradition. Stephen was conflicted. In one ear he heard his sacramental theology professor saying, "Baptism is for the living, not for the dead." In the other, he heard his pastoral care professor saying, "The sacraments are not ours to withhold." He was confronted with a moral and practical pastoral decision. How should he proceed in order to stay faithful to the tradition which recognized him as a minister and, at the same time, care for a woman who asked him to act as an agent of God in the world?

Stephen's experience is not unusual. Taking his experience at face value, I asked questions of how to teach students of ministry how to navigate this all too familiar terrain. As a theologian shaped by a highly sacramental and liturgical view of the world through Roman Catholicism, this practical question of ministry nagged at me. I went to the library stacks.

I read professional publications from chaplaincy associations. I dove deep into Catholic moral handbooks that were used to prepare priests for their pastoral vocation. I conducted an ethnographic study with hospital chaplains to gather their collective practical wisdom. I wrote pastoral prescriptions based on the research.

I found answers, but I remained unsatisfied. I wrote about "women," essentializing a category of experience that I knew was far more complex. Although I heard stories of particularity in identity, and the repercussions of living in a world which is biased and unjust because of perceptions of who one is, my writing to the question of care in ministry did not take up the most complex pieces of the puzzle: the constellations of identity which we inhabit and which inhabit us; the relationship between personal and social suffering; and of course, the pastoral theological question of what caring ministries look like when they are justice oriented.

During the time that I was exploring this question intellectually, I found myself invited to become an other mother to my newborn niece. I dove heart first then head into co-parenting, traveling to Bolivia, a developing country in South America, where the questions of recognition, suffering, subjectivity, and social justice confronted me from all sides. Holding my niece, I waited to climb aboard the S *micro* (bus) from *la Zona Sur*, a poor, indigenous residential neighborhood with limited access to food, pharmacy, and healthcare, and ride 30 minutes to the city center of Cochabamba. During the ride we passed by a few vegetable stands, the *tiendita* where I walked to buy bread and chocolate from the storekeeper, Marcela, and a mural on cinderblock that declared *"No es un juego"*—"This is not a game"—and depicted people standing at attention at the end of a bomb.

My questions on recognition became visceral when I looked at my part Quechuan daughter—full head of brown hair, brown eyes, and brown skin, even at one month. I asked myself many questions as I reflected. How am I to care for this new life so as to create the intrasubjective and intersubjective conditions for her to thrive and flourish? As an indigenous mestizo and Euroamerican person, a female, a citizen of both Bolivia and the United States of America, what may she experience as a result of her visible and invisible identities which may cause her harm as a result of racism, colonialism, and sexism? How will she be perceived by religious or social communities in North America which uphold heteronormative and Western visions of marriage as a theological norm for parenthood and childrearing? Through no particular choice of my own, except to respond as best as I was able in love and care to the vulnerable creatures who inhabited my life, including myself, I saw all that was at stake in the developmental task of recognition as well as the social and theological implications.

## Recognizing Other Subjects

Theories of recognition describe the psycho-social-theological process by which selves receive recognition. Recognition is the capacity, ability, and willingness to see another person as they are and as they hope to become. As an intersubjective process, asserting one's needs and receiving recognition of those needs is part of the work of guiding and nurturing human development for growth and transformation. Practicing assertion and recognizing another's assertions begins in primary relationships when as infants we must trust that those to whom we have been entrusted care for us and love us in all that we are and all that we hope to become, taking into account our unique personalities, our social identities, and circumstances and histories that we are born into without necessarily giving our consent. As a social process, recognition is critical to create a more just society. Recognition of one's identity through social and political systems is the means by which legal rights are advanced. Recognition as a theological process is grounded in the claim that every existence is a graced existence. As a graced existence, we claim that God is present with us and accompanies us in our journey as embodied spirits and inspirited bodies. Theologically, when we optimally recognize another self-in-relation, we practice how to love another in freedom.

Not all recognition is optimal. We are misrecognized or not recognized at all. As such, recognition is a risky task. At every turn, we must place ourselves in the hands of another and trust that they will respond in love and care oriented toward our maturation. Likewise, we reach our hands into other's lives. As infants and children, we have no choice but to trust that our primary caregivers want the best for us as they are able to imagine and see the world. As adults, placing ourselves in another's hands is terrifying particularly when we are people already hurt and frail, people who believe that we are not yet capable of cultivating wholeness. Healing from these wounds requires acknowledging our finitude and brokenness as well as imagining health in a register that includes failure to recognize. Margaret Kornfeld comments, "We are learning that health is not just the opposite of illness: health is the consciousness of one's wholeness—and that means accepting one's limitations as well as one's strengths."[1]

Not only are we terrified of what might befall us through our personal relationships, as we mature we come to understand that what our bodies reveal—not always with our permission—may also bring us harm by larger society. We wear our social and theological identities on our person and ask that we be recognized as a self of value who ought to be free from violence and harm. Sometimes, our bodies betray us. The color of our skin and the swish of our hips makes our bodies legible to social, political, and religious institutions which can recognize us, misrecognize us, or not recognize us at all. We act to receive recognition, sometimes receiving misrecognition or non-recognition instead. We may contort our bodies and our self-perceptions as we search for or demand recognition. Contortions may become intersubjective disfigurements of domination and submission. We can come to love our oppression and subjugation because we also receive the very thing that we desire: recognition. We cast parts of ourselves outward, making them abject and other, including constructed but real social identities. We fear our embodiment. Institutions, including family and church, wield the tools of systems of power that brand us: flint knife, tattoo needle, billyclubs, handcuffs.[2] We may not remember being wounded until our scars pulse with pain, the skin inflamed, where misrecognition or non-recognition has inscribed itself and cast out our living flesh.

As the people of God, we need balms, sutures, and medicines of all types to heal the wounds. Recognition is one medicinal remedy in ministry. Ministry claims the goodness *and* the brokenness of the world. In pastoral recognition, we respond in care to repair, mend, and make whole while acknowledging both the goodness and brokenness. In the context of pastoral theology, theorizing about recognition assists us to more fully understand the complexity of subjectivity. From there, our pastoral tasks of healing and caring, and also resisting, liberating, transforming selves and community, and cultivating the capacity for self- and communal-determination, are grounded in a pastoral reflection which more adequately accounts for subject formation. Theorizing recognition

1. Kornfeld, *Cultivating Wholeness*, 8.
2. Certeau, *The Practice of Everyday Life*, 141.

also implicates institutions in the maintenance of social injustices and petitions for prophetic action for social change.

Attending to theories of recognition is critical for the cultivation of pastoral wisdom on lived subjectivity. My argument begins by acknowledging that we live within a constellation of identities in which we may be recognized, misrecognized, or not recognized, both at all and at any given time. As such, we ought to examine the importance of recognition across the intersubjective, social, and theological spectrums. The problem of recognition which I describe is also its answer: recognition. Seeking pastoral wisdom on recognition draws us toward "a wider vision for the practice of love" in feminist pastoral theology.[3]

## Methodological Context

I situate this inquiry in the context of feminist pastoral theology. I examine theories of recognition from a feminist perspective, taking up questions of suffering, subjectivity, and social justice along the way. I also pay particular attention to gender and sexuality. As third wave feminists, womanists, and queer theorists have noted, typically paying attention to gender has assumed race (white) and class (middle, at least). Hence, my discussions within this book are situated in light of 3rd wave feminist critiques. As such, I attend to the importance of gender at the intersections of race, sexuality, coloniality, and ability as much as I am able, given the confines of the text and the hopes for communicating clearly. Methodologically, I utilize a revised critical correlational method where pastoral theology and resources from cognate disciplines are brought into dialogue with each other to theologically reflect on lived experience.[4] In this book, I am in conversation with three major figures to reflect on recognition: Jessica Benjamin who brings a feminist psychoanalytic perspective; Judith Butler who brings a critical social theory perspective; and Marcella Althaus-Reid who brings a liberation theology perspective. Additionally, I reflect on the lived experiences that I have encountered personally and in contexts of ministry.

3. Ramsay, "Contemporary Pastoral Theology" 155.

4. Tracy, *Blessed Rage for Order*, 43. Within pastoral theology see also Browning, "The Past and Possible Future of Religion and Psychological Studies"; Doehring, A Method of Feminist Pastoral Theology"; and Miller-McLemore, "Cognitive Science and the Question of Theological Method."

As a feminist scholar-practitioner living at the porous peripheries of modernity and post-modernity, I am aware of the importance of inhabiting self-reflexivity as a situated knower. I have built a knowledge portfolio that has both strengths and weaknesses based on what I have experienced, what I have not experienced, what I will never experience, and what I can only imagine experiencing. I trade knowledge using currencies drawn from the modern ethos of universal emancipation and the postmodern ethos of asking which power and whose emancipation.

The particularity of postmodern knowledge claims is important to the enterprise of pastoral theology. Pastoral theologians are called to account for the power that they hold through social identities or locations, such as race and ethnicity, class, gender, ability, religion, sexuality, age, and education. Pastoral theologians must be explicit about how their locations impact the shape of the knowledge they build and acknowledge how their location is shaped by power.[5] One accepted way to be explicit is to name one's social location. I am deeply grateful for the fortitude and courage that women and men in pastoral theology have exhibited in proceeding in this manner,[6] especially when naming a location is also a "coming-out as" process.[7] However, I also resist this form. I am too wary of confessions that feel coerced, of new norms of liberative practice that enslave persons in old economies of knowledge, of difference that solidifies and mutates into deviance. I am wary of asking social locations to do too much work without questioning the shape of our revealed and revealing knowledge. Social theorists Rogers Brubaker and Frederick Cooper comment, "If identity is everywhere, it is nowhere."[8] The onus is to communicate what might be conveyed through identity or social location without lapsing into extensive memoir or autobiography, while also acknowledging the incompleteness and tensions of every narrative. In fact, this observation is central to my argument.

5. Neuger, "Power and Difference," 66.

6. See the foreword to feminist pastoral theologian Joretta Marshall's *Counseling Lesbian Partners*, where Andrew Lester acknowledges his gratitude "to Joretta for taking the personal risk inherent in writing this book" (ix).

7. I use the phrase "coming-out as" to denote, first, that naming and claiming an identity is not a one-time process, but one in which a person comes out again and again. Second, I use this phrase to denote how an identity may become crystallized for us, even when we see our identity as something much more fractured.

8. Brubaker and Cooper, "Beyond 'identity,'" 1.

So, I tell you as I can, as succinctly as I can, of my social location and how it informs the shape of my research. I have no doubt that I have already revealed things about myself to you in writing thus far and also by what I have not written. No doubt, many more tensions in my personal narrative and my pastoral theological concerns will emerge. For now, I tell you the following formations: I am a white woman. I grew up without memorable ethnic influence in proximity to the Beltway, the major highway that encircles the District of Columbia, the capital of the United States of America. I am most familiar with the Roman Catholic religious tradition, and also find myself comfortable in many places beyond the ecclesial institutional church. I have been privileged to enjoy extensive education opportunities. I situate my research interests at the broad intersection of theories and practices of care and justice. I worry about domination and submission, subtle coercion, and psychological manipulation in everyday practices of caring because they are mistaken for love, for justice, for mercy, for healing. Working out of a feminist, pastoral, and theological framework, I intend to engage my sources with theological virtues of prudence, generosity, respect, and humility. I hope that those who engage this work will also act in the same spirit.

## Chapter Overviews

This book offers a way to understand the importance of recognition as a process central to human development and growth. Because of the importance of recognition, I argue that pastoral theologians must understand how recognition, misrecognition, and denial of recognition work on individual psyches, between people, in our social and political lives, and in our theologies and their praxis. As such, I have organized the book attentive to these locations of recognition.

In Chapter 1, "The Challenge of Identity," I argue that recognizing another subject is difficult work but is central to pastoral praxis and theological reflection. Further, I show that the framework of identity, while helpful to a point, is also limiting. When pastoral theologians reflect on ministry, an uncritical use of identity can be used to mask experiences of oppression and subjugation, or to fix a subject's experience by appealing to identity. Because feminist pastoral theologians care about justice and because we seek to act justly as we care, I argue that theories of recognition offer a rich counterbalance to the limiting effects of an identity framework alone.

In Chapter 2, "Feminist Pastoral Theological Anthropology," I argue that feminist pastoral theologians have laid the groundwork for rich engagement with theories of recognition as they relate to subject formation. I dialogue with Joretta L. Marshall, Carroll A. Watkins Ali, Elaine Graham, Barbara J. McClure, and Pamela Cooper-White as feminist pastoral theologians who articulate theologies of subject formation. They do so by attending to women's experience and human experience from feminist commitments to enable human flourishing. I outline their work in order to systematize the significant depth and breadth of feminist theological anthropology attentive to lived experience. I am critical of the role of recognition in their narrative constructions and conclude that recognition is a critical framework for constructing subjectivity.

In Chapters 3, 4, and 5, I describe the capability and need for recognition, as well as the consequences for when those needs go unmet, through psychoanalytic theory, social theory, and liberation theology. In Chapter 3, "Intersubjective Recognition," I argue that intersubjective recognition is a key need in human development and growth, providing strength that enables a self to be in relation with another self. When optimal recognition is unmet, selves-in-relation settle for counterfeits, including patterns of domination and submission. In this chapter, I use an extreme example, reading *The Story of O* with Jessica Benjamin, a feminist psychoanalyst. *The Story of O* is a story of sexual submission and domination in which the circuit of recognition and assertion is warped, having us mistake subjugation for love. Consequently, subjugation is reproduced within family life from generation to generation. I conclude that without attention to intersubjective processes of recognition hopes for social transformation will also remain unfulfilled.

In Chapter 4, "Social Recognition," I argue that our complex identities also must be recognized by social and political systems. Like a constellation, our complex identities are distinct points that form something which is interpreted as being visible, and thus then cited. Citing our identities make us legible to others and to social and political systems. However, legibility can also include erasure or marginalization, making the way we and others cite our identities matters of life and death. Drawing from queer theorist and social critic Judith Butler, I argue that our performed identities are sites of both playfulness and potential hurt. When we play out our identified becoming, systems of power, and those subject to them, can give us a yes, no, or maybe even as we assert ourselves. A yes, no, or maybe carries consequences both for the giver and the receiver. I offer the work of mourning as a practice that calls forth the conditions for intersubjective and social recognition.

In Chapter 5, "Theological Recognition," I argue that subjectivities of persons outside the normative visions of sexual desire and gender performance are misrecognized or not recognized at all within theological discourse. Dialoguing with the provoking work of Marcella Althaus-Reid, a liberation theologian writing through a queer theory lens, I argue that sustained inattention to non-heteronormative lives damages our ability to develop adequate descriptions of subject formation. I describe Althaus-Reid's unique contribution toward a methodology for a liberative epistemology of theological recognition, and conclude with her that learning to love indecently is critical to recognition of complex subjectivity.

In Chapters 6, 7, and 8, I develop pastoral theological responses to the challenge of identity in light of the problem and solution of recognition. In Chapter 6, "Recognizing Injustice," I argue that enacting a just care practice attentive to identity requires us to develop the affective capabilities for lamentation and confrontation. I describe how structural violence and political repression are places where assertions of self and group identity are muffled and silenced. When this happens, pastoral theologians call on the embodied practices of lamentation and confrontation. Rather than introjecting our sorrow or aggression, we channel these reactions out of the body and into the public sphere so that the self and communal resilience is cultivated.

In Chapter 7, "Encountering Other Subjects," I outline key facets of a feminist pastoral theology of recognition and describe a theo-praxis of encounter. Because we are habituated in our giving and receiving of accounts of ourselves and other selves, and because we are habituated in feeling and interpreting our situations and the situations of others, I argue that social geography is a critical tool for pastoral theology. Social geography calls theologians to account for what they hold to be physically and spatially off-limits. I argue that a failure to encounter those things which have been deemed off-limits is problematic in enacting a pastoral praxis of recognition. As such, I offer the image of the street journalist.

In Chapter 8, "Recognizing the Self-in-Relation," I give my account of a self-in-relation constituted by co-becoming. Writing from my ground of experience, I reflect on giving untamed accounts in describing subjects, and the role of blessing in the project of co-becoming. I close with a spirituality of mutual beholding through which we learn postures of receptive action where we might see the loveliness of another subject, and not a subject who is Other.

As a final introductory word, allow me to emphasize that recognition is a desire of the human heart. Recognition paves the way to love, which is a theological, spiritual, and pastoral good. Yet, we know that to simply claim love is not good enough for pastoral theology. In Christian theological language, we experience and participate in personal and social sin, both by omission and by commission. Claims of love, which have proven constrictive rather than liberative, have caused harm to the people of God and deformed selves. My goal in this book is to broaden perspectives of feminist pastoral theology in relationship to identity and recognition so that we continue to enable flourishing in our theologies and their praxis. I wish to advance a care that does justice. For what is theologically at stake in recognition is the question of how to participate in our graced becoming and the graced becoming of Others, even while acknowledging the vicissitudes of sin and suffering. In this book, I do hope that you find that I have taken up these questions as living questions. Further, I hope that you will do the same.

# 1

## The Challenge of Identity

No person gets out of life without experiencing suffering. Intuitively, those seasoned by the school of hard knocks know that grief and anguish are present in everyday life. We experience injustice, material and relational poverty, and violence enacted upon us without having given our consent. How ought feminist pastoral theologians reflect on and respond to these life conditions by which we are shaped, and which we also may shape? I answer that recognition is a key framework with which feminist pastoral theologians must grapple.

Right from the start, examples help to concretize heady concepts. Annually on November 20, transgender activists and allies remember the lives of transgendered people who have been murdered because they are, or *appear to be*, transgendered. A list of names and how they died is read aloud. While some names are known, others are not: unknown woman, stoned to death and skull crushed; unidentified woman, severe head injuries and body thrown under a truck; unidentified child (13 years old), hung.[1] Violence and death meet these women. Lives are undone. They are met with injustice because of the perception of their bodies and identity. The transgendered woman who is beaten to death is misrecognized or not recognized by her aggressors. She is a man masquerading as a woman, not a "real" woman. She, or he in the aggressor's mind, has broken

1. Abernathey, "Memorializing Transgender Day of Remembrance 2013," lines 19–23, 35–39, 47–51.

13

normative gender codes. In the exchange, she asks to be recognized as a woman. Her aggressor denies her recognition. The aggressor's revulsion leads to her violent death. At her death, her name is unknown, her story is largely unknown, and recognition is refused. How ought feminist pastoral theology reflect on her story? What mechanisms enable feminist pastoral theologians to hear her story and in her own voice? Do we have adequate frameworks to account for her complex subjectivity? How ought we care justly?

Allow me to phrase these sets of questions in another way. Given that subjectivity is complex, layered, and constellated, and given that personal and social suffering are experienced in ways that are difficult to pull apart, to point toward singular root causes, and even to speak of, what resources enable and cultivate the capacity to enable the telling of stories of subjects—of persons co-becoming in relationship to themselves, others, and the Divine—which do not fit current frameworks which construct subjectivity?

In this chapter, I argue that recognizing complex subjectivity is difficult work in feminist pastoral theology, and that the work is limited by the construction of a framework of identity. The use of a framework of identity necessitates categorization even as observation of subjectivity increases in complexity beyond what any category might be able to hold. Said another way, "women's experience" is complex and problematized by class, race, ethnicity, ability, coloniality, sexual desire, anatomy, and religio-spiritual orientation. Attention continues to grow around the complex diversity of lived experience, and this is critical. However, claiming identity can be a norm-making project, masking privilege and concealing important experiences of marginalization within communities.[2] This observation is particularly problematic for pastoral theologians in two ways.

2. Crenshaw, "Mapping the Margins," 1242. Crenshaw uses the term intersectionality to describe the problem that identity politics "frequently conflates or ignores intra group difference" (1242). In her pivotal essay, she examines how battering and rape of black women are "the product of intersecting patterns of racism and sexism," and yet "tend not to be represented within the discourse of feminism or antiracism," leading to further marginalization (1243). She writes, "[W]hen the practices expound identity as 'woman' or 'person of color' as an either/or proposition, they relegate the identity of women of color to a location that resists telling" (1242). Inattention to intersectionality results in institutional and public policies which harm women of color even while aiming for the empowerment of women more generally.

First, attention to identity is important, but it is not a panacea to understand the full complexity of subjectivity. In some sense, the discipline of pastoral theology has always understood this, drawing from psychology and social sciences to gain insight for use in caring and healing the world. However, identity is the framework par excellence currently, organizing much of the literature that defines feminist pastoral theology in the last decade. And for right reason: identities, which are never fully under our own singular control, which are visible, less visible, and even invisible, are intertwined with experiences of oppression and marginalization.

Second, groups of people experience suffering based on some aspect of their identity: transgendered women who are beaten to death in Brazil; Palestinian children who will not be remembered in their lives or their deaths; physically disabled Haitian men who eke out a subsistence in Port-a-Prince; religious leaders who dare to risk a caring response in the face of structural violence. Suffering is embodied and lived with. Suffering is identified with an aspect of the self—nationality, gender, race and ethnicity, sexual desire, ability, religious identity—which may limit recognition of the complex interwovenness between structural violence and personal suffering. Feminist pastoral theologians ought not be constrained by current frameworks of identity in recognizing the manifestations of suffering and pain. While identity is a starting point, accounting for subjectivity—that is, the ways that we are made and that we make ourselves under both constraint and freedom—demands that we investigate the framework of identity for the ways it disables and enables giving and receiving complex accounts of subjectivity and suffering, as well as the possibilities for hope and transformation.

This chapter proceeds by attending to feminist pastoral theology as a specific location of constructed subjectivity. My argument proceeds in three steps. First, I ground the discipline and practice of pastoral theology as an inquiry into subjectivity deeply rooted in the conceptual frameworks of the living human document and the living human web. I also introduce the phrase *selves-in-relation* as another way to capture the existential subject of feminist pastoral theology.[3] Next, I argue that caring, justice-making, and understanding lived experience through identity are

3. In his groundbreaking book *The Relational Self*, Archie Smith, Jr. argues that correlating social ethics and psychotherapy in pastoral contexts is critical for personal and social transformation. My use of self-in-relation springs directly from his rich contributions.

braided practices in feminist pastoral theology. Last, I argue that a deeper understanding of recognition is one tool needed in the caring and healing of selves-in-relation.

## Grounding Feminist Pastoral Theology in Subjectivity

"Pastoral theology has always looked to the parishioner, the believer, the suffering, and the practices of religion as central resources in the search for theological answers," write the editors of *Feminist and Womanist Pastoral Theology*.[4] Pastoral theology and pastoral ministry are rooted in concern for the human person, her suffering, and her flourishing. In other words, pastoral theology reflects on and theorizes about subjectivity, drawing from the deep wisdom of caring with selves-in-relation. While I argue that feminist pastoral theology *already* theorizes about subjectivity, I would also like to suggest that renewing deliberate discussions about subjectivity in light of theories of recognition are critical to advance the field. To do this, I describe the aim of pastoral theology in order to reflect on the development of theories of lived subjectivity.

Before reflecting on subjectivity, I will give shape to how I understand pastoral theology and feminist pastoral theology. Feminist pastoral theology is an area within pastoral theology that uses gender as a primary lens for analysis. My comments center primarily on pastoral theology, as feminist pastoral theology arose as a response to a limited worldview in pastoral theology. Pastoral theology reflects on ministry, context, process, and practice. However, at the root of pastoral theology is concern for a contextual self, a self-in-relation, although the scope of the context—a cone that begins with intrapsychic forces and expands to familial, cultural, socio-political, and even ecological forces—has not remained static. Studying the self-in-relation in light of theological claims leads to complex, contested, and multiple aims of pastoral theology and its practices. However, four preliminary observations structure how I understand pastoral theology given its roots in premodernity and its current location on the cusp of modernity and postmodernity.

First, pastoral theology is a reflection on the activity of pastoral care, and the situations that stimulate the need for a caring response. Second, contemporary pastoral theology, while aimed toward contextuality and

4. Miller-McLemore and Gill-Austern, "Introduction to Feminist and Womanist Pastoral Theology," 11.

diversity, cannot be divorced from its historical Christian roots in offering normative visions of flourishing through pastoral practices of care, vis a vis moral guidance, ecclesial wisdom, and practices of faith. Thus contemporary pastoral theology sees many viable forms of flourishing in individuals from its pre-modern roots, but remains committed to addressing issues that stem from a modern commitment to the struggle for human liberation in a pluralistic, global world. Third, this very commitment leads to a broadening of the scope of care. Pastoral theologian Nancy J. Ramsay observes that pastoral theology has increasingly become concerned with the "wider public horizon for care."[5] As such, "this wider horizon has meant that pastoral theologians now find themselves developing normative proposals for public policy debates on issues affecting care in our common life such as welfare and family policies."[6] Fourth, pastoral theologians and religious leaders reflect on how to be leaven in the world to address harms in society and church, and draw on resources far and wide to do so.

Pastoral theology developed from Christian liberal theology's embrace of modernity, which uses reflections on subjective-life and secular resources to ask and answer theological questions. Liberal theology, informed by both mainline Protestantism and Roman Catholicism, opened the door to changes in both scholarly and liturgical life. Protestant thinkers like Paul Tillich (1886–1965) and Rudolph Bultmann (1884–1976) developed new threads for intellectual development drawing on resources and methods from secular thinkers. For example, Tillich developed a method of correlation to explain "the contents of the Christian faith through existential questions and theological answers in mutual interdependence."[7] Bultmann sought to demythologize the New Testament in order to provide new means to reflect on kerygma and the nature of faith. In Roman Catholicism, the Second Vatican Council (1962–1965) famously engaged the question of how to be Church in the modern world, a pastoral question that Pope John XXIII answered with the simple term *aggiornamento* or updating the church. Updating resulted in major liturgical and theological shifts, such as the use of the vernacular language of a region rather than Latin in liturgy.

5. Ramsay, "Contemporary Pastoral Theology," 157.

6. Ibid.

7. Tillich, *Systematic Theology*, 60.

In the discipline of pastoral theology, modernity and subjective-life is brought into relief with Anton Boisen's call to study "living human documents rather than books,"[8] and Bonnie J. Miller-McLemore's clarification and expansion from human as document to "living human web."[9] As terms of subjectivity, both living human document and living human web represent the existential nature of pastoral theology, a discipline which deliberately invites reflection on complex, and yet innovative and integrated ways to think and act in light of the vicissitudes of life. The discipline has suggested pastoral tasks that assist in creating responsive care environs: healing, guiding, sustaining, reconciling, nurturing, liberating, resisting, and empowering.[10]

Terms, aims, and tasks point toward the production of lived theories of subjectivity. Existential concern for the person in practice, not only theory—psychological, theological, pastoral, social, or otherwise—grounds pastoral theology in its self-understanding and its methods of practice.[11] However, practical concern for the subject is descriptive as well as prescriptive, and here lies the rub. Because practical prescription is grounded in the description of situational realities of suffering as well as fulfillment, it behooves us to consider the nature of description of the self-in-relation. Thus, enacting theory in the real world and theorizing from the real world requires a certain attentiveness to methods of inquiry, particularly as scholars become increasingly aware that theologies and praxes that seek to liberate, heal, and care may also sustain the very conditions that reify inequalities, marginalization, and oppression. Because description of subjectivity—that is, of the living human web—is vital to pastoral theology, we must examine our predominant lenses, paying special attention to identity as a central lens that we use to organize the feminist pastoral literature of subjectivity.

While I have alluded that pastoral theology already participates in reflecting and formulating theories of subjectivity, I have yet to define

8. Boisen, *Exploration of the Inner World*, 10.

9. Miller-McLemore, "The Living Human Web," 16.

10. Healing, sustaining, guiding, and reconciling as pastoral tasks were identified by Clebsch and Jaekle in *Pastoral Care in Historical Perspective*. Nurturing was identified by Howard Clinebell in *Basic Types of Pastoral Care and Counseling*, 43. Carroll A. Watkins Ali advocated empowering and liberating in her text *Survival and Liberation*, 129. Resisting is cited by Bonnie J. Miller-McLemore in "Pastoral Theology as Public Theology," 62, and "The Subject and Practice of Pastoral Theology," 181.

11. Miller-McLemore, "Practical Theology and Pedagogy," 185.

subjectivity in relationship to pastoral theology. Allow me to do so at this juncture. A theory of subjectivity is a theory of the human person in the social-political context set against qualifications of agency, power, psychological formation, and social construction. Approaches to subjectivity fall along a wide spectrum in describing a subject's ability to effect individual and social change, and to resist institutions and practices that oppress. Subjectivity builds toward a complex account of pastoral theological anthropology that sees care through a justice lens. Seeing the person, her dignity and worth, her capacity for self-transcendence and participation in the goodness of life, is spiritual work. Spiritual work, as liberationists like Gustavo Gutierrez have taught us, begins by identifying forms of oppression that are similar to and break from past iterations. When we consider subjectivity within a pastoral theological framework, we are invited to reflect upon the nature of subject formation, particularly as pastoral theology attends to the events, circumstances, and identities by which the self-in-relation is shaped and also may come to shape. Rejecting epistemological positivism in formulating and responding to lived theories of subjectivity, pastoral theologians deploy praxeological inquiry as they construct theories which aim toward phronesis, prudence, or practical wisdom, particularly in the context of ministry.[12] Practical concern for the self-in-relation is the heart of pastoral theology.

## Uses of Identity in Pastoral Contexts

So far, I have argued that one of the tasks of pastoral theology is to reflect on and develop theories of lived subjectivity, doing so in order to ascertain how best to critically accompany a self-in-relation as she seeks wholeness and healing. I deliberately choose this phrase—critical accompaniment of a self-in-relation seeking wholeness and healing—to indicate the expansive possibilities inherent within a reflective praxis of feminist pastoral theology. As pastoral practitioners dare to risk a caring response, their praxis necessitates attention to the complex intersection of caring with justice-making and with the uses of identity. This has implications as to the practice of pastoral care, encouraging pastoral theologians to

12. Browning, *A Fundamental Practical Theology*, 3. Browning describes how religious communities are carriers of and contributors to practical reason in this book. His argument hinges on understanding communities made of practitioners of faith as embodiments of practical wisdom (10). Also see *Religious Ethics and Pastoral Care* for an earlier synopsis.

expand the conceptions of what healing-caring ministries might look like: conversation, counseling, ritual, place-making, community development, social entrepreneurship, public advocacy, and more. While I would suggest that pastoral activities as caring ministry is expansive, this expansion is indicative of the turn to intersectional identity as a framework. We use identity in order to pinpoint how oppression is uniquely manifested in complex experiences of multiplicity while also living out theological claims about who God is and what the human-Divine relationship invites the human community to move toward.

The work of identity hides and shows, veils and unveils, makes and unmakes, builds and unbuilds our theologies, our institutions, our practices, and our very selves-in-relation, which may be places of liberation, transformation, cherishing, self- and communal-determination, and self- and communal-blessing, but which also may not be these things. For every reclamation of a term, like that of "queer," words like "retard" and "fag" continue to be used to stigmatize and marginalize selves-in-relation. Already, I hope it is becoming apparent that we are challenged in giving accounts of ourselves when we begin from a framework of identity because we never know exactly how our identities are perceived and how they might be used for us and against us, blessing us with recognition and also reconstituting us through violent social structures and practices. It is precisely from the observation that oppressions have been masked because of inattention to the complexity of identity that identity emerges as a central paradigm for doing just care. My intention in what follows is to show how identity and just care are at work in feminist pastoral theology. I argue that feminist pastoral theologians have linked injustice through the lived realities of identity as means of further refining theories of lived subjectivity, and begin to hint toward the difficulties in giving accounts of oneself in this context.

Caring and justice-making are interrelated activities in pastoral theology, as the authors of *Injustice and the Care of Souls: Taking Oppression Seriously in Pastoral Care* make evident. The collection speaks to the growing conversation about what it means to take oppression seriously in pastoral care. The authors answer that oppression-sensitive pastoral care pays attention to marginalized persons in their contexts and communities. As a corollary, caregivers must also pay attention to their own privileges and internalized oppressions to witness to a care that does justice.[13]

13. Kujawa-Holbrook and Montagno, *Injustice and the Care of Souls*, 1–2.

Overall, the tome invites direct pastoral theological engagement with wider and more complicated issues of structural violence and oppression, and challenges easy dichotomies between care and justice. Yet, further reflection is needed in order to imagine how we might care justly without reifying theoretical divisions between care and justice.

In social-political theory, there are ongoing conversations around care and justice which give context to the state of pastoral theology. The normative epistemological mode in social-political theory has posited the terms and practices care and justice as oppositional and dichotomous. When the debates between justice and care are played out, they break over fundamental descriptions of the state of human nature. Deeply influenced by utilitarian and Kantian deontological ethics, the assumed norm of human life is subject as autonomous, rational, and self-interested, and as such our social and political structures reflect this assumption and affect how we advance justice. A necessary correction is that of a care perspective, emerging from feminist social and political theorists, which claims the state of human nature as one of care. Simply put, we are born, live, and die in a horizon of care, and as such our social-political structures ought to account for these realities. As Monique Deveaux explains,

> The underlying message of the care perspective is as powerful as it is succinct: put briefly, it states that human relatedness and the practices that support it shape us in profound ways. It also states that taking this fact seriously in political terms would precipitate fundamental changes in our social arrangements.[14]

A care perspective begins from the central assumption that we are selves-in-relation. While this perspective precipitates profound shifts in social-political structures, it also necessitates even more profound shifts in our theologies and practice of life together. Because relatedness is central to the human experience, feminist pastoral theology is a discipline central to the reflection and development of theology capable of unmasking ideologies and practices which harm selves-in-relation.

The liberal paradigms of justice are precisely those that care perspectives challenge. The assumption is that care is about personal relationships, the family, friends, and charitable organizations while justice is about the public sphere, the political, economics, and capital. The critical care perspective argues that dividing justice and care in such a way is harmful and denies what feminists have long noted: that the personal is

14. Deveaux, "Shifting Paradigms," 115.

political. Virginia Held comments, "Feminist analyses have shown how faulty are traditional divisions between the personal and the political . . . We can see how unsatisfactory it is to assign justice to public life and care to private."[15] Deveaux reminds us that there is no "need to match liberalism concept for concept."[16]

In the life of the church and the writings of pastoral theology, care and justice are not nearly as dichotomous, although divisions do exist. The traditions of the social gospel, public theology, and social movements, like the civil rights movement of the 1960s or the sanctuary movement of the 1980s, were fueled by an interstitial approach to care and justice based in theologies of liberation. Pastoral theology's interface with liberation theology expanded the focus of pastoral theology from practices that are therapeutic in nature to social-political and policy driven practices of intervention and caring.[17]

However, addressing the person and society at the same time is a difficult task. Pastoral theologian Bonnie J. Miller-McLemore writes, "Current problems in sustaining a public voice for pastoral theology go right back to an effort that, with Walter Rauschenbusch's immersion in New York soup kitchen ministry, once joined social ethics and pastoral care as two sides of the same coin."[18] The problem with two sides of a coin is precisely that balancing on an edge requires that the coin be in motion to show both sides. Thus, caring for women requires addressing gender injustice. Caring for families requires examination of public policy that contributes to hardship or disintegration of families. Caring for persons of color or an ethnicity different than that possessed by the caregiver provokes personal and social critique of oppressive forces and stereotypes, and their subsequent internalization and social repetition.

Identity is an important paradigm for feminist pastoral theology because it shows how personal suffering is, in part, constructed through social structures, how exclusionary patterns of thought are made normative, and how oppressive practices vis a vis public policy and ecclesial policy are maintained by overt or covert machinations related to one's identity. Feminist pastoral theology begins its analysis by attending to gender and specific cases of marginalization and exclusion. Analyzing

---

15. Held, "The Meshing of Care and Justice," 128.

16. Deveaux, "Shifting Paradigms," 117.

17. Lartey, *In Living Color*, 113–39.

18. Miller-McLemore, "Pastoral Theology as Public Theology," 53.

through identity reveals the operation of injustice and the need for care attentive to oppression. However, the problem of identity is precisely its use: it can obscure or stymy the liberatory aim of doing just care.

For our purposes, identity is defined as multiple and competing forces that shape how women (and men) experience the world. Identity is not the whole and sum of a person. A subject's very being and formation cannot be boiled down to gender, race, ethnicity, sexuality, or the intersection of multiple identities. As second wave feminists remind us, identity is not *only* something deeply personal, but also something deeply political. Our identities are not neutral territory. They can be used by us and by others in ways that denigrate our lives, ignore our lives, or flourish our lives. As such, identity as attributes of one's person ought to be considered through the paradigm of difference rather than diversity or multiculturalism.

The word difference refers to the inequalities that one experiences as a part of one's diversity. Summarizing postcolonial theorist Homi K. Bhabha, pastoral theologian Pamela Cooper-White writes that diversity is a liberal value distinct from difference. She explains,

> The former [diversity] perpetuates an idea of consensus in which difference is tacitly contained and controlled by the dominant culture; the latter [difference] is "based on unequal, uneven, multiple, and potentially antagonistic political identities," multiple identities that "articulate in challenging ways, either in progressive or regressive ways, often conflictually, sometimes even incommensurably—not some flowering of individual talents and capacities." [19]

Identity is inseparable from difference. The interplay of differences allows for the production of one's own identity as set apart from that of another person's identity. As a process, recognizing difference does not guarantee that all identities are tolerated, much less celebrated. At the extreme, identity converts difference into irreconcilable otherness, making a person an alien, a monster, or a demon. At the scale of politics, the challenges of identity and difference raise concerns for the practices of

19. Cooper-White, *Many Voices*, 45.

democracy[20], justice-making[21], and caring, particularly in the context of feminist pastoral theology.

Feminist pastoral theology uses identity as a means to describe and probe how a subject is formed. Examining the effects of identity on a subject's being and becoming provides the basis for theological reflection and pastoral action. However, attention to identity alone does not guarantee just care. The history of the development of feminist and womanist pastoral theology bears witness to the need for correctives to assumed norms of just care. That is, feminist pastoral theology developed as a corrective to the assumed norm of a male-oriented approach to care. Later, womanist pastoral theology developed as a corrective to the assumed norm of a white woman-oriented approach to care. Both developments indicate an opacity which prevents practitioners and scholars from fully seeing patterns of harm at the social level and their presence at the familial, intersubjective, and intrapsychic levels. For feminist pastoral theology, identity ought not become the good in itself. Rather, it must be a means to understand the things that impede our flourishing, to discover new places of resilience, hope, metanoia, and transformation, and to reflect on our being and becoming in all its complexity.

## Recognition, Misrecognition, and Non-recognition

It has been my contention that a slavish attention to identity may obscure the nuances of personal and social suffering, as well as our deep

20. Connolly, *Identity\Difference*, x. Connolly argues that attending to the relationship between identity and difference in democratic theory necessitates a move toward "agonistic democracy" which "affirms the indispensability of identity to life, disturbs the dogmatization of identity, and folds care for the protean diversity of human life into the strife and interdependence of identity\difference."

21. Young, *Justice and the Politics of Difference*, 3. Arguing against a theory of justice as universal and comprehensive (for example, that of political theorist John Rawls), Young develops a critical theory that accounts for difference in light of injustice. She explains that everyday discourse about justice makes claims that exceed the boundaries of a universal, self-enclosed justice theory. She writes, "They are instead calls, pleas, claims *upon* some people by others. Rational reflection on justice begins in a hearing, a heeding a call, rather than in asserting and mastering a state of affairs, however ideal" (5). As such, a theory of justice which denies difference (e.g., a Rawlsian veil of ignorance) or which presupposes mastery of process leads to justice (e.g., the distributive paradigm) ignores how social structures or institutional contexts influence which social groups receive privilege and which social groups continue to experience domination and oppression.

formation by others and our deep forming of others. Identity, like structural violence and like social injustice, is relational. That is, my identity is not something already set in stone, permanent, unchangeable. On the contrary, it is in contexts of relationality, of being and becoming, that how I perceive myself and how I am perceived by others may shape my self- and other-understanding. Further, we tend to think that structural violence and social injustice are outside the parameters of relationality, but I would like to suggest that this is not the case at all. Instead, we ought to think about structural violence and social injustice as being deeply rooted in relational matters. Hence, dismantling the violence of our lives will necessitate relational repair.[22] To be sure, there is no one antidote to remedy the complex problems of structural violence and social injustices which precipitate our need for care, particularly as they manifest around our social and personal identities. However, I believe that studying theories of recognition are what make possible wiser and more nuanced understandings and articulations of the self-in-relation. Cultivating practical wisdom on lived subjectivity makes room for another to participate in her own co-becoming with greater awareness of the deepest formations, having exited from and being returned to her own self's graced existence.

In what follows, I begin to outline what I mean by recognition, attentive to the psychological, social, theological, and pastoral realms. Additionally, know that these realms also intersect, crossover, borrow, inform, and operate in each other's realms. There are no hard lines: "The personal is philosophical is political."[23] An understanding of recognition deepens what we understand just care to be. An understanding of recognition also tells us something about how to create conditions of just care, particularly given the difficulties of identity frameworks. At the very same time, let me emphasize that recognition is not a panacea, either. Subjects may be misrecognized or not recognized at all. This is the challenge that I described at the beginning of this chapter when I spoke about the transgender woman whose embodied presence in social space shows how her identity was used to denigrate, and ultimately destroy, her life.

It helps to start with introductory definitions for recognition, misrecognition, and non-recognition. First, recognition is an intersubjective exchange between a subject and another subject, institution, or system of

22. Sharp, *Misunderstanding Stories*, 15.
23. Kittay, "The Personal is Philosophical is Political," 393, 407.

power/knowledge, including a theological system of power/knowledge. It is a psychological phenomena, a social and political phenomena, and a theological phenomena. Our asking to be recognized begins in our first days of life as we cry when we're hungry, cry with a dirty diaper, or cry when we're overtired. Our mothers, fathers, or other primary caregivers respond to our assertive cries, recognize our physical needs, and attend to those needs, as they are able. Of course, our physical needs are prescient of our emotional and spiritual needs in the course of our human development.

Not all primary caregivers are made equal, however. While parental failure is necessary for development, not all failure is optimal. British child psychologist Donald Winnicott describes the good-enough mother who does not respond "perfectly" every time. She, or another primary caregiver, does not respond to every cry of the infant and thus the infant feels frustration. He writes, "If all goes well the infant can actually come to gain from the experience of frustration, since incomplete adaptation to need makes objects real, that is to say hated as well as loved."[24] Though not perfect, primary caregiver failures to respond are optimal, and through the process the infant learns that the primary caregiver is separate from the infant's self, although still related. That infant's self, through optimal failure, is assisted in developing and structuring a self capable of a full range of emotions, including both love and hate. Further, that self becomes capable of trusting itself. Winnicott's concept is helpful to understand optimal recognition from an intersubjective perspective. When failures are less than optimal and are also continuous, children may be deterred in the development of self. This may result in either misrecognition or non-recognition. To suffer from misrecognition or non-recognition at the individual level as an infant or young child results in challenges to the development of one's self-determination capabilities as a self matures and thus affects the capacity to be a self-in-relation.

As a social phenomena, recognition, particularly of one's identities, is critical to full participation in social and political life. Political theorist Axel Honneth argues that "the justice or well-being of a society is proportionate to its ability to secure conditions of mutual recognition under which personal identity-formation, hence self-realization, can proceed adequately."[25] One need only think of certain groups of people who have

24. Winnicott, *Playing and Reality*, 11.
25. Fraser and Honneth, *Redistribution or Recognition?*, 174.

been denied social recognition historically, particularly through rights, access, or participation, to understand more fully: African-Americans and voting rights; same-sex couples and marriage rights; and persons with physical disabilities and rights to physically access places. Following from Honneth, social recognition makes room to consciously rethink and redesign institutions, public policy, justice-making strategies, and practices of care for the self-in-relation in order to enable the flourishing of all.

Recognition is not a linear process as it must also include failure through misrecognition and non-recognition. Doing just care requires a capability to grapple with the linkages between interpersonal and social recognition. While interpersonal recognition makes capabilities of self-determination possible, social recognition makes possible parity of participation and, ultimately, social justice. Parity of participation requires "all to participate as peers in social life" based on "the principle of equal moral worth."[26] Parity of participation is critical for all persons, but especially for groups of people denied, historically or currently, rights, access, or full participation because of a critical non-normative identity: sex, gender identity, sexual identity, race, ability, religion, socio-economic class, nationality, or ethnic origin. A society without the means of achieving parity of participation is an inherently unjust society. As critical theorist Nancy Fraser writes, "Overcoming injustice means dismantling institutionalized obstacles that prevent some people from participating on par with others, as full partners in social interaction."[27] As such, the tasks of economic redistribution and political representation must be accompanied by social-cultural recognition in order to advance social justice.

When persons are denied social recognition based upon a group identity, they are subject to mistreatment and oppression. Doing just care requires *recognizing the need for recognition* in order to unthread the misperceived or unseen structural violence written into the narrative of our lives. In *Justice and the Politics of Identity*, Iris Young proposes that oppression must be understood as having multiple faces in order for us to recognize it as oppression. She identifies the five faces as exploitation, marginalization, powerlessness, cultural imperialism, and violence, and argues that categorization by this system allows us to see more clearly who is oppressed and how she is oppressed. The categories of oppression

26. Fraser, *Scales of Justice*, 16.
27. Ibid.

are plural so as to avoid a "one group" phenomenon, e.g. all women, and show that experiences of injustice are both incredibly personalized as well as structural. She explains, "Social theories that construct oppression as a unified phenomenon usually either leave out groups that even the theorists think are oppressed, or leave out important ways in which groups are oppressed."[28]

Narratives of personal suffering are indicative of larger manifestations of social suffering. For example, our nameless, Brazilian transgender woman is subject to personal violence—one-on-one violence at the hands of a person or a few people—and to structural violence—violence at the hands of social, political, and theological systems. Let us extrapolate what little we know and assume that she did not die the first time she ventured into the public streets and stores. Instead, her presence elicited multiple opportunities over time, in multiple communities and spaces to experience optimal recognition, misrecognition, or non-recognition. She herself did not crumble, dissolve, or dissipate the first time she was subject to marginalization, alienation, or disenfranchisement, no matter which theory of justice we use to analyze her experiences. Rather, it was by repetition that she experienced less than optimal recognition. At her death, she experienced non-recognition and condemnation from another who claimed that she was not due the right to live and acted in ways harmful to her human dignity.

In that moment of encounter between two subjects, how do we interpret her response to less than optimal recognition? Is she a passive subject? Perhaps, even as she was beaten to death, she resisted, clawing at those who wielded the sticks and stones, and shielding her head and her kidneys. She asserted her agency, her right to resist, and the dignity of her human life. This kind of extrapolation lays bare a fundamental problem and paradox of misrecognition and non-recognition at the social level. Misrecognition and non-recognition contribute to mistreatment and oppression, and at the same time, may also give rise to personal and social agency. The site of harmful subject formation can also be the site of resistance. But not without cost. Repeated patterns of misrecognition at the level of individuals leave a counter-residue at the social level. Likewise, repeated patterns of misrecognition at the social level leave a counter-residue at the level of the psyche-soul and throughout theological discourse and praxis.

28. Young, *Justice and the Politics of Difference*, 63.

Social misrecognition, then, is associated with a particular identity group such as gender, ability, or race. At one end of the spectrum, social misrecognition may be a process by which those who possess institutional power overlook another group. At the other end of the spectrum, social misrecognition may be an othering process whereby groups of people are expelled entirely from public discourse and viewed as less than human. In the middle of the spectrum, we may find a "conscious acceptance" alongside an "unconscious aversion" toward persons whose identities are understood as being visible.[29] For example, we know that xenophobia, racism, sexism, heterosexism and homophobia, ageism, religious intolerance, and ableism are very much alive. Some, like heterosexism, are more explicit and socially-politically legitimated than others, like racism and sexism. Those who care for and care about oppressed, marginalized and misrecognized people are obliged to identify "contemporary manifestations of group oppressions."[30]

Feminist pastoral theologians must account for how personal suffering and social suffering are inextricably intertwined, what role theology plays in misrecognition and non-recognition, and how pastoral theology might inform a more liberative theory of subjectivity. Theological recognition as critical lens takes as its starting point experiences of marginalization and oppression that are experienced within ecclesial systems, maintained by theo-linguistic systems, and blessed as divinely ordered systems of exclusion and marginalization. Any list of examples may already arise in your mind: the leadership role of women in the Christian tradition; the question of blessing same sex marriages; the continued ableism that pervades our churches in Scripture, liturgical acts, and the physical structures that disable community gatherings in which all may participate. Black theologians and ethicists, womanists, feminists, queer, postcolonial, and liberationists of all religious stripes have pointed out how theological systems require redress. Studying injustice that manifests in both social and ecclesial spaces through a lens of recognition tells us the *what* of justice that necessitates attention and diligent care. Additionally, we learn from a psychic-social perspective *why* injustice is perpetuated and how we might make long-lasting corrections that repair society and the human heart. Theological recognition, like interpersonal and social recognition, proceeds in a system. Individuals and groups of

29. Ibid.,130.
30. Ibid, 131.

people may be misrecognized or not recognized at all, even within emancipatory oriented theological systems.

Pastoral recognition, then, is oriented toward constructing more
adequate theories of subject formation and to advocating for recognition in multiple spheres of the world. Pastoral recognition can also be
marked by misrecognition and non-recognition. Even optimal pastoral
recognition, like interpersonal recognition, must include failure. Not every pastoral care interaction will be "perfect." This rings true for feminist
pastoral theologians who have acted as care agents even while perceiving
that some critical aspect of another subject's identity or life history is at
work without explicit knowledge of this identity or history. Pastoral recognition is uniquely oriented toward perceiving the holy within another
self. As such, pastoral recognition is an invitation to deepen a spirituality
informed by justice, care, and love while also making room to encounter
other selves in ways which may be aggressive or mournful.

In sum, recognition is a critical category of human experience which
effects the movement toward a liberating interpersonal, social, theological, and pastoral space. Recognition is a process over time involving multiple agents. The intersubjective exchanges which occur over time build
libidinal, or psychic, energy between subjects who may participate in
optimal recognition, misrecognition, or non-recognition. Many activities aim toward the recognition spectrum, including activities which do
harm to subjects like domination and submission, violent beatings and
death, and marginalization, as well as activities which assist in human
flourishing, like loving, caring, nurturing, liberating, and decolonizing.
In short, recognition is both challenge to growth and place for growth. It
is where we may encounter Divinity, self- and other-blessing, and transformation, and where we may continue to be subject to ignorance, violence, and suffering. It is where our being and becoming is constituted.

## Why How We Describe the Feminist Subject of Care Matters

I've contended that how we describe the feminist subject of care matters,
and further that attending to recognition from intersubjective, social-
political, and theological frameworks is critical to advance a care that
continues to be oriented toward liberation and justice. However, recognition is a highly theoretical category, as are care and justice. As such, allow

me to offer a brief case study to ground the problem of subjectivity and recognition.

I introduced the minister-theologian Stephen in the previous chapter. When he reflected on his pastoral ministry, he posited the goods of pastoral theology as in conflict with the goods of doctrinal theology. At the heart of his conflict, namely whether he should baptize a stillborn fetus, was not only a personal moral quandary, but also a question about the purpose of ritual in pastoral caregiving. I turned to hospital chaplains to gain wisdom on how they administer ritual and pastoral care to women (and their partners and families) when a fetus is non-viable. They offered sage advice in moral-decision making, but as I listened I was struck by what I did not hear. Most of the women were working-class or impoverished, self-identified as female-bodied, heterosexual, non-U.S. citizens or legal immigrants from the global south and Eastern Europe, and identified with a highly sacramental religious sensibility. Some spoke no or limited English. In reviewing this data I had expected to hear chaplains comment on the intersection of identities and how it might affect ritual caregiving and its reception. Chaplains noted identity markers but said little to contextualize how to care for vulnerable and marginalized persons in their contexts. On the other hand, I found a plethora of feminist pastoral theological literature that prescribed care based on a highly contextualized identity framework, but did not adequately hold in tension the dynamics of justice, care, ritual, and identity.

Still, I wrote my findings. I described three distinct moments in moral-decision making in ministry. First, chaplains ought to gain clarity. Chaplains ought to know departmental hospital policy regarding baptism of non-viable fetuses and infant death, particularly if serving in a hospital with a clear religious affiliation. Chaplains ought to also know intimately their own tradition which recognizes them as a minister as well as have a base knowledge of other traditions' view of ritual. Second, chaplains ought to maintain clarity. They should have a clear understanding of ritual acts and their purpose. They should be able to articulate their theology of baptism and theology of ritual, gesturing toward sources of authority, whether culled from scriptural, theo-intellectual, ecclesial-institutional, or practical sources. Last, chaplains ought to enact clarity. Chaplains ought to clearly convey to bereaved parents the nature of the ritual offered. Do not tell grieving parents that a child is receiving the sacrament of baptism when a naming and blessing of remains is enacted.

Ritual dishonesty breeds is sinful. It is neither compassionate nor genuine care.

While my arguments for clarity were quite practical, my discomfort grew. I thought about domination, structural violence, and what it means to advance a care that does justice, liberates, and empowers. My problems originated in the descriptions of women. Yet, all my answers centered on the responses of the chaplains. Additionally, religious identity took center stage while other identities of difference fell by the wayside. Though robust, the body of pastoral literature did not sufficiently address the problem of identity that I saw. From this case, I concluded that what is needed is a more robust development of how our descriptions of care may be limited by who we can see as a fitting subject of care. I saw theories of recognition as a tool of discernment.

I believe that theories of recognition are a powerful tool to develop more robust accounts of subjectivity. They provide the how and why of subject formation which leads to more precise articulations of the what and who of suffering. In the next chapter, I review and appreciate five feminist pastoral theologies of subjectivity to show that recognition is central to development of a more adequate theory of formation of the self-in-relation.

# 2

## Feminist Pastoral Theological Anthropology

More can always be said in any account we give of the self-in-relation. We know by way of experience that any telling of our lives is always incomplete, whether we are reflecting on specific cases of identity that call for recognition as a pastoral intervention for doing just care, or extrapolating from specific cases to larger theological claims about subjectivity. While many accounts in theology remain to be told, feminist pastoral theologians have historically created and held open space for complex accounts of subjectivity. They have actively reflected on the formation of the subject through feminist and womanist lenses. Some, like Joretta Marshall and Carroll Watkins Ali, have offered implicit theories of subjectivity by attending to the complexity of identity, suffering, and injustices. Others, like Pamela Cooper-White, have articulated theological anthropological visions of the person. Each of these authors progressively refines our understandings of subjectivity and barriers to flourishing, beginning with heterosexism (Marshall), racism (Ali), and sexism (Graham), moving to social constructivism (Graham, McClure, and White), and extending to multiplicity in theological anthropology (White).

My intention in this chapter is to provide an appreciative inquiry into the state of subjectivity in feminist pastoral theology by engaging these five authors on their own terms. Furthermore, I engage them in order to systematize feminist theological anthropologies attentive to care and lived experience. To accomplish this, I show how they construct their

theologies of lived subjectivity and reflect on the tasks of pastoral theology in light of those constructions. I contend that each author offers
significant contributions to thinking about subjectivity, but they have not
attended to the dynamics of recognition explicitly. Without attention to
these dynamics, care for the living human web is distanced from critical
analysis about the formation of persons through identity and the machinery of oppressive systems that judge and condemn based on one's identity
and performance thereof. Hence, claims for just care may be misrecognized or not recognized at all if identity as the framework *par excellence*
is not carefully considered in light of what it hides and shows. In order
to make way to cultivate a critical consciousness attentive to recognition,
we turn to distinct voices who theologize about women's experience and
human experience from feminist commitments.

## Subjectivity and Sexuality

Tending to diversity and difference is one route of reflection on subjectivity and is widely accepted in feminist pastoral theology. However, it is
important to remember that this paradigm that encourages reflection on
diversity was not always so. Courage was, and continues to be, required
in the face of internalized and socially constructed institutions, practices,
and thought patterns of oppression, marginalization, and exclusion. For
this reason, the publication of *Counseling Lesbian Partners* by Joretta L.
Marshall was and remains an important contribution to pastoral theological reflection on subjectivity and sexuality.[1]

   At the most fundamental level, Joretta Marshall argues that lesbian
individuals are complex subjects who, first, are not deviants from a God-
given heteronormative sexuality, and second, are deserving of supportive
pastoral counseling because God affirms human sexuality that is covenantal. She writes, "Women in lesbian covenantal partnerships reflect the
church's normative understanding of relatedness and are to be affirmed
and blessed by God and the church."[2] Further, Marshall explains that

---

   1. See reviews by Nancy J. Ramsay in *Journal of Pastoral Theology* (7:1) and James
I. Higginbotham in *Encounter* (60:1) for examples of how *Counseling Lesbian Partners*
was praised for its substantive and courageous contribution.
   2. Marshall, *Counseling Lesbian Partners*, 14.

God desires that the covenant between oneself and God-self be enriched through relationships of love, justice, and mutuality.[3]

Marshall offers us a thick theological anthropology of human development and partnership. She does not shy away from human brokenness in individual development or in the context of relationships. As a result, Marshall offers us a rich theology of subjectivity by issuing a vision of life together as women-loving-women, but not one which is idyllic or which might ever be free of the pains of patriarchy, sexism, or heterosexism. Thus, she holds in tension the call to support partnerships of love, justice, and mutuality as the telos of human sexuality, while describing how challenges to a woman's understanding of herself as a lesbian arise from internal and external sources.

First, Marshall argues that the claiming of a lesbian identity is a challenge, though one that leads to liberation, spiritual depth, and possibilities for deeper relationships of mutuality and care. She draws on clinical psychologist Vivienne Cass to provide a six-step developmental frame for identity emergence: identity confusion to identity comparison to identity tolerance to identity acceptance to identity pride to identity synthesis. While Cass asserts that these stages are linear, Marshall disagrees, writing, "I would suggest that they be seen as fluid and dynamic interpretations women bring to their self-understandings at different points in their journeys. Often a movement from one perspective to another is met by resistance, fear, or lack of support, making it difficult to fully embrace what Cass describes as the qualities of a given stage."[4] "Fluctuation and shifts" and identities that "may be experienced as long-lasting but are not necessarily fixed and permanent" are part of the formation of a sexual orientation, and a key component of a lesbian's sense of self. Thus, part of Marshall's theology of subjectivity includes a sexual and embodied self who is in-process. Marshall's use of language of self-identifying, while also being identified by others, or "naming and being named,"[5] also implies the relational nature of her theological anthropology. As well, it implies a sense of coming to know who one is and having that identity positively reflected by another individual.

Second, Marshall presents specific challenges to covenantal lesbian partnerships in the forms of addiction, lesbian battering, sexual abuse

3. Ibid.
4. Ibid., 35.
5. Ibid., 38.

survival, and fusion in relationships. She notes that these challenges are not unique, "but they can be the most common and overlooked struggles in these relationships."[6] While she focuses on the intrapersonal dynamics between the challenged partners, Marshall demonstrates how to carefully excavate and examine personal histories and social norms that weaken partnerships of love, justice, and mutuality. Additionally, she shows us how to use all the data available to make wise assessments and do goal-setting in counseling relationships. For example, she gives the case of lesbian battering in the couple Jane and Phyllis. They have engaged in verbal and physical combat with each other, with Jane as the perpetrator of domestic violence and Phyllis as the victim. Marshall's description of the situation fits the typical understanding of domestic violence, with the important exception that it is woman to woman. She writes, "The most common misconception in working with lesbian partnerships is that women do not hit other women and that battering is not present in the lesbian community . . . Physical violence between women does exist and reckoning with this reality is imperative so as not to minimize abuse when it does occur."[7] By making a claim like this, Marshall also shows us that her theological anthropology does not assume essentialist feminine qualities of caring and tenderness as constitutive of gender identity. Instead, a woman can be violent and aggressive, emotional states which may be due to internalized images of "women as victims or as unhealthy persons."[8]

Lastly, Marshall's emphasis on assessment, goal-setting, and proactive pastoral care reveals a theological anthropology where relational injustices are reflective of social injustices and thus must be encountered within oneself and within larger social structures. She presents the case of Sara who is an executive director of a new pastoral counseling center. Sara and the board grapple with whether they ought to reach out by placing an advertisement in the lesbian and gay newspaper in order to grow the center. They worry what the reaction from the denominations that support the center might be. Marshall uses this case to state explicitly that the theological call to build community necessitates inclusion of marginalized voices.[9] To refuse to do so is to collude with silencing and to believe

6. Ibid., 70.

7. Ibid., 78.

8. Ibid., 79.

9. Ibid., 128.

FEMINIST PASTORAL THEOLOGICAL ANTHROPOLOGY

that the church has nothing to do with injustices that arise from lack of access to resources of care. However, to break silence also requires that pastoral care specialists do inner work to identify their own homophobia.

To sum up, by attending to lesbian partnerships in all their strengths and weaknesses, and as part of the divine gift of human sexuality, Marshall offers pastoral theologians and care specialists a rich theological anthropology that, though focused on lesbian identities, has a wider reach. First, she reminds us that developing a sexual orientation is always a process, and one negotiated at an interpsychic and intrapsychic level. Second, she shows that a woman-loving-woman can embody hyper-masculinized qualities of control, physical aggression, and rage. Third, while sexism, homophobia, and patriarchy are forces that impinge on the psychic and spiritual health of individuals and couples, Marshall shows us that persons have the ability to resist and to create loving, just, and mutual relationships, sometimes calling upon assistance from pastoral care specialists to help in resistance to oppressive forces.

Marshall's work is pivotal to developing and sustaining a line of questioning that challenges heteronormativity in Christian religious traditions and practices. Marshall reminds us that coming out may be a liberative and challenging process "that upsets the status quo and moves the world off-center."[10] Her work offers a pastoral apologetic for caring about women in homosexual relationships. In light of the conservative streak of the recent U.S. religious landscape, which responded with a "love the sinner, hate the sin" thematic approach, or demonizing desire and naming the homosexual as patient in need of *cure* from wrong desire, e.g. reparative therapy, Marshall puts into literary flesh a liberal pastoral theology that dialogues with emergent psychological scholarship on supporting lesbians while deploying Christian theological concepts to bolster her claims. Yet, more is needed in thinking pastorally about how a subject is formed in relationship to her sexuality. For example, how might our descriptions of subjectivity and pastoral care be amplified by taking account of an intersectional analysis of lesbian sexuality and race?[11] As

---

10. Ibid., 104.

11. Douglas, "The Black Church and the Politics of Sexuality," 349. Douglas writes, "While the Black Church community is arguably no more homophobic than the wider Church community or heterosexist society of which it is a part, causal observations do suggest that it is perhaps more unyielding and impassioned than other communities when expressing its anti-gay and anti-lesbian sentiments."

we advance a field that cares about justice, we will continue to need to expand our approaches to sexuality as a critical site of identity formation.

## Subjectivity and Racialized Injustices

Womanist pastoral theologian Carroll A. Watkins Ali brings complex questions of racial injustice to pastoral theology. Like Marshall, she describes the pastoral theological subject with implications for care. Questions of subjectivity arise as she describes the limit situations that affect psychological and social health for African-Americans. As a womanist pastoral theologian speaking on subjectivity, as well as a womanist offering a contextual pastoral theology, she offers a unique view that accounts for subject formation by multiple identity markers and a collective history that makes visible racially insensitive pastoral care and theology. Further, she remains hopeful that pastoral interventions may restore a subject's own sense of self.

Ali writes out of her own cognitive dissonance as a student of pastoral theology and a black woman. She asks how pastoral theology might build "a conceptual framework . . . in the African American context that is adequate to the struggle of many African Americans to stay alive and be free of the oppression of racial injustice."[12] With this in mind, she leads us into the depths of human experience through the accounts of Lemonine, Pauletta, and Doris. She notes that these stories are to illuminate and speak to the collective whole about survival and liberation.

Ali's significant contribution to a pastoral theological anthropology is an account of the difficulties of surviving systematic racial injustice coupled with crippling social and psychological suffering. She briefly highlights the legacy of cultural loss through the transatlantic slave trade, the blindness of history that overlooks black women's resistance, classism and racism vis a vis unequal pay and work opportunities, the systematic racism that supports hard-to-break cycles of crime and violence in impoverished black communities, the workings of the prison-industrial complex, and the familial stressors of alcohol and drug abuse that maintain "genocidal poverty."[13] The stories of Lemonine, Pauletta, and Doris tell us about the process of becoming a subject in the face of survival

---

12. Ali, *Survival and Liberation*, 1.

13. Ibid., 25.

against genocidal poverty. I recount Ali's vignettes next as they are demonstrative examples of pastoral theological subject construction.

In her first biographical sketch, Ali tells us the story of Lemonine. Lemonine was a black woman who passed as middle class, but struggled to support her two children and her one grandchild as a single mother. She experienced racism at her workplace, worried about paying for medical care, worried that her car would be stolen by gang members or would need major repairs, worried about paying rent. Her multiple and intersecting jeopardies of class, race, and gender shaped her to strive toward being a strong matriarch for the family, striving which landed her in the hospital for debilitating exhaustion. "Truly," Ali writes, "*life* was Lemonine's presenting problem. There are no other diagnoses in the traditional sense."[14] She "was basically suffering from being overcome by her own personal life, while trying to cope with all the external social realities that affected each age group of her family members."[15] She was the strong black woman who suffered by trying to hold together that which social structures of oppression would tear asunder.

But Lemonine was also a savvy woman, and though she could not afford therapy she found in Ali someone who would work with her despite her inability to pay the full fee. Meeting with her for three years, Ali primarily offered Lemonine supportive therapy. Ali writes, "Each weekly session during our relationship served mainly to build Lemonine up enough so that she could go back out to face a hostile world for another week."[16] But this was not enough to reverse the cumulative life trauma and its psychological toll on Lemonine. Ali reports that Lemonine became more and more hopeless: "I witnessed Lemonine lose hope and give up on life altogether."[17] Six months after therapy was mutually terminated, Lemonine died of a brain tumor.

In her second biographical sketch Ali describes her caring efforts with Pauletta. Pauletta was a single black mother and poor. She came to Ali to mourn the death of her first-born teenage son, a victim of gang violence. He was shot for wearing "the wrong colored hat," a wrong doing which had occurred seven years previous to Pauletta's therapeutic

14. Ibid., 5.
15. Ibid.
16. Ibid.
17. Ibid.

encounter with Ali.[18] Session after session Pauletta grieved the loss of her first-born, and "the dynamics of her own personal life."[19] Loss of support engulfed Pauletta. Her younger son joined the army and church folk from whom she had drawn strength in the midst of her crisis seven years ago were tired of hearing about the tragic loss of her first-born son.

Ali offered her supportive therapy and the space to grieve and cry out her anguish. "The purging went on session after session, but it was what she needed. That was not what was needed to solve her problems, but there was an enormous amount of grieving that Pauletta had to come to terms with before she could move on with her life."[20] After all, "Life as a Black female had by no means been easy," Ali writes.[21] By grappling with feelings of loss, abandonment, and isolation, Pauletta made positive strides in her life. Ali concludes by sharing that Pauletta had found work as a community activist and was doing "fairly well."[22]

Lastly Ali shares Doris' story with her readers. Doris was a black woman who grew up in a home filled with physical and emotional abuse. Her mother justified the abuse by reasoning, "I would rather beat my own kids to make them act right, than for them to get beat out in the street by White police."[23] Doris internalized this fear of violent external patriarchal and sexist systems as self-hatred and abused drugs and alcohol. Her health was poor, Ali reports. Further, all the kinds of jobs that her education and training qualified her to do—minimum wage and physically taxing work—were not manageable given her poor health. Doris also had two children who were both deaf. Seeking public aid for her family, she came under the watchful eye of the social work system. The "System," as Doris called it, was an aggressor that fed off her fear with threats to prove her inadequacies as a mother, even though her skill as a translator between the children and the case workers, ironically, demonstrated her commitment to caring for them.

Doris was referred to Ali when her court-ordered therapy group terminated. Ali makes the point that Doris was resistant to seeing anyone besides a black woman. When donated funds ran out to pay her fee,

18. Ibid., 131.
19. Ibid.
20. Ibid., 132.
21. Ibid., 131.
22. Ibid., 132.
23. Ibid.

Ali continued therapy with Doris because "the issues were too serious to drop."[24] She reports,

> In reality, Doris spent most of her time at home child-rearing, in the silence of two deaf children, trying to negotiate the "System" and struggling with poor health, while people (even church people) and family distanced themselves from her and her children. I could see that Doris, despite all that she had been through, was still trying to overcome the odds without any real support. Doris was virtually alone.[25]

In these three vignettes Ali compassionately shows how systematic injustices contribute to the material and psychological conditions of genocidal poverty. Genocidal poverty limits Lemonine, Pauletta, and Doris in monumental ways. They are unable to move with freedom in their social and psychological worlds. In sharing their stories, Ali reveals her implicit theory of subjectivity. She accounts for some agency of the subject, but this agentic power also meets with extreme resistance in multiple forms: from friends, family, and church who ought to care, but can no longer do so; from social systems that ought to help, but are unable to effectively do so; and from intrapsychic forces where unfulfilled desires for hope and belonging morph into despair, isolation, and grief.

To Ali, the dire conditions of African-Americans are a critique of the pastoral shepherding model proposed by pastoral theologian Seward Hiltner. In *Preface to Pastoral Theology* (1958), Hiltner argues that the discipline of pastoral theology reflects on the ministerial activities of healing, sustaining, and guiding within his proposed shepherding perspective. Ali critiques Seward Hiltner's shepherding perspective in three ways. First, she argues that his shepherding model is paternalistic and overvalues the pastor's perspectives. Second, his individualistic approach is representative of white European American cultural thought, and presumably a male rationality. Last, the pastoral operations he proposes—healing, sustaining, and guiding—are culturally insufficient for the current situations of African-Americans. Ali offers additions to the pastoral functions in nurturing, empowering, and liberating.[26] She writes,

> In general, guidelines for the pastoral care of African Americans from a womanist perspective call for the expansion in character

24. Ibid., 133.
25. Ibid.
26. Ibid., 121.

and content of the ministry described by Hiltner's shepherding perspective. In terms of the character of ministry, the womanist perspective offers two guidelines in addition to Hiltner's call for an "attitude of tender and solicitious concern." The first order of business . . . is . . . urgency . . . Second, the attitude of pastoral care should also be one of advocacy that is embodied in action.[27]

The realities of the African-American experience necessitate urgency and action on the part of pastoral caregivers. A shepherding perspective is too passive in the face of cultural genocide. Action is required.

Ali's expansion of the pastoral functions and her critique of Hiltner gives us insight on how ministry can lead to critical accounts of subject formation. She argues that the Black church must engage in the practices of ministry—preaching, pastoral counseling, Christian education, youth ministry, and community outreach—to give hope while in the midst of struggle.[28] Because Ali is not explicit, we must draw some conclusions on our own. Namely, the tasks of Christian ministry in form and in content are practices of resistance to a dominant cultural formation that leads to nihilism and genocidal poverty for African-Americans. In this sense, Ali holds open a space for a changing self-perception of self and others in community, and is adamant that liberation cannot come at the expense of denial of one's culture.

It is outside the scope of her book to explicitly describe a theology of the person and her formation, yet I believe that Ali has done so, attentive to subject formation through the evils of racism, classism, and sexism. Resisting either/or thinking, she maintains hope that practices of pastoral ministry might intervene in that same subject formation. Still, what might it mean to deepen our understanding of subject formation in light of her insights? As I recounted above, the case studies of Lemonine, Pauletta, and Doris are representative figures of the suffering that black women undergo. In order to care more justly we must also examine how descriptions intended to liberate may unintentionally reinscribe harmful stereotypes of black women.[29] What might it mean to read the story of Lemonine, the female head of household who died from exhaustion, through an analytic lens that accounts for the harms of the matriarch

27. Ibid., 136.

28. Ibid., 154–61.

29. Collins, *Black Feminist Thought*, 76–93. Collins identifies the controlling images of the jezebel, welfare queen, mammy and matriarch and describes their historical development and current forms.

image and tries to trace these harms concretely as they become visible in Lemonine's family life and her interpretation of faith claims?

As a controlling image, the matriarch is the strong black woman given to bouts of anger. She drives men away through her unchecked aggression and her unfeminine personality emasculates her male lovers and husbands. Her children are without fathers because she will not conform to the appropriate and ideal gender behavior. Thus, she must become the breadwinner, as well. Sociologist Patricia Hill Collins writes, "In this context, the image of the Black matriarch serves as a powerful symbol for both Black and White women of what can go wrong if White patriarchal power is challenged. Aggressive, assertive women are penalized—they are abandoned by their men, end up impoverished, and are stigmatized as being unfeminine."[30]

Womanist pastoral theologian Teresa Snorton identifies two relational locations where the matriarch stereotype thrives and describes the harm that the image causes. First, the controlling image is reproduced intergenerationally. Mothers covertly teach their daughters the skills of survival, namely strength and independence, so that they too are able to be care leaders for their own households.[31] Snorton explains, "Often the lessons are so covert that one might miss them, except for their telling impact on how one is expected to respond to life's difficulties."[32] Second, an insidious incarnation resides in the pastoral exultation of that image. In the wake of deep suffering, the matriarch is a woman of strong faith, one who cries out to God for healing and prays for the Holy Spirit to revive her soul. Snorton writes, "She has many problems; however, traditions of faith and culture have taught her that her only recourse in this life is to look Godward."[33] In the middle of crisis, she testifies to the saving power of God while others look to her for words of comfort.

I raise the question of the shape of Ali's case studies in order to advocate for fuller accounts of subject formation. Accounts of cultural histories are critical to advance liberative paradigms of pastoral theology. Her accounts of material poverty and the psychological state of her clients are descriptive, giving voice to women like Pauletta, Doris, and Lemonine. However, descriptions are not analysis. Analysis must

---

30. Ibid., 85.

31. Snorton, "The Legacy of the African-American Matriarch," 55.

32. Ibid., 55.

33. Ibid., 54.

challenge oppressive systems, including pastoral systems, that cultivate nihilism and genocidal poverty in black women's lives. Analysis may also reveal the shape of agency available to subjects. Without analysis within the context of these case studies, stereotypes may be reproduced unintentionally. As a result, an account of racial subjectivity may become distorted and border on misrecognition of black women.

## Subjectivity and the Post/Human

Elaine Graham, Samuel Ferguson Professor of Social and Pastoral Theology at the University of Manchester, explores the post/human condition in the monograph *Representations of the Post/Human: Monsters, Aliens, and Others in Popular Culture* (2002). The term post/human connotes a trajectory of thought resulting from a genealogical method. She examines the discourse of Western technoscience and popular culture for representations of human identity. She writes about a large range of scientific and cultural material and thinkers, from the Human Genome Project and Star Trek to Donna Haraway and Luce Irigaray, working each thoroughly to show the face of humanity that is refracted through the mirror of narrative. She explains,

> In analyzing the representations of selected post/human figures—liminal characters, inhabiting the boundary between the human and the almost-human—I have resisted essentialist models of 'human nature', preferring instead to emphasize the way in which definitive versions of what it means to be human emerge from encounters with the refracted 'Other' in the form of the monster, the android, the *Doppelgänger*, or the alien.[34]

Using a genealogical approach, Graham shows us that current preoccupations with what becomes of the human subject in light of multiplying cybernetic, biomedical, and digital technologies is a question that is part of the mythos of the "purity and fixity"[35] of human nature, or what Graham terms "ontological hygiene."[36] The result of her study is a deconstructive theory of the person that builds on "representation, monstrosity

---

34. Graham, *Representations of the Post/Human*, 221.
35. Ibid., 36.
36. Ibid., 11, 33–35.

and alterity, contingency of human identity, and the resurgence of the sacred."[37]

It is important to situate her most current study within the trajectory of thought exemplified by her previous scholarship on gender and practice in postmodernity. In *Making the Difference: Gender, Personhood, and Theology* (1996), Graham embarks on a multi-disciplinary study of gender to develop a theology of gender. She engages anthropology, biology and psychoanalysis to teach her reader about normative theories of gender. Once she has accomplished this task, she interrogates theories of gender through detailed accounts of how bodies are disciplined to social norms, not exemplars of a free form anthropology of gender; how what is "natural" is challenged in the bodies of intersex or transsexual persons and thus reveals the social construction of the "natural;" and how essentialist understandings of gender expel difference in order to stabilize themselves. Her contribution in this book is not only a thorough account of gender theory and its debates, but also a movement toward a theology of gender that "must engage with the pluralism and complexity of interdisciplinary theories of gender at a profound level."[38] Further, her scholarship locates her reflections squarely within pastoral theological reflection on subjectivity.

In her book *Transforming Practice: Pastoral Theology in an Age of Uncertainty* (1996), Graham develops an account of pastoral theology as a "critical theology of Christian practice" that addresses the postmodern challenges to identity, power, and knowledge.[39] She argues that understanding pastoral theology as "critical phenomenology of pastoral practice" lays the groundwork for a postmodern pastoral theology.[40] In this form of pastoral theology, the grand narratives and "eternal" moral norms of faith communities that shape practice are not absolutized and ahistoricized, but evaluated and investigated in light of "the complexity of human experience and their viability as public and communitarian forms of practical wisdom."[41] She grounds her conclusion by way of observation of transformative feminist praxis that issue from the sources and norms of women's experience, faith traditions, and the community of

---

37. Ibid., 225.

38. Graham, *Making the Difference*, 222.

39. Graham, *Transforming Practice*, 3.

40. Ibid., 209.

41. Ibid.

faith. She offers feminist preaching, feminist spiritual direction, and liturgy as women-church as concrete examples. Again, her contribution in this demanding text is a depiction of the implications of postmodernity for ecclesial communities. In light of her future work in post/humanity, *Transforming Practice* is a critical study that attends to how ecclesial practices might be understood as sites for engaging difference and alterity.

In *Representations of the Post/Human,* Graham extends her scholastic reflections on personhood, alterity, and the postmodern turn by engaging cultural studies as a locus of theological reflection. Her concerns are framed better as a reflection on subjectivity when we ask her text what we ought to be wary of when constructing a theory of subjectivity. She answers that we should be aware of four factors in constructing theories of the person: representation, monstrosity and alterity, contingency, and resurgence of the sacred.

First, we ought to be wary of representation as a stand-in which displaces the original with a simulacrum. Graham gives the example of the human genome project which becomes the "code of codes"—that which distills the wild diversity of humanity by discovering the exact sequencing of four proteins: cytosine, guanine, adenine, and thymine. Decoding of the human person problematically effaces the actual person, but at the same time leads to questions of power and authority. If the code is only partially representative of human diversity, as scientists are increasingly coming to believe, then who has the power to speak for whom? Further, "representations that are ideological or reductionist—humans as genes, machines, nature as feminized other—serve to enshrine and reify certain assumptions about normative and exemplary humanity, but at the expense of excluding others from the discourse altogether."[42] At stake in representation is the question of who has the authority to determine what and who is legitimately human, and the potential to repress or oppress that which is deemed alien or monster.

Second, we ought to be aware of the ways in which human creatureliness is reconstructed as alien or monster. Graham examines monstrosity, or teratology, as a discursive site on boundaries and identity. Examining *Star Trek* as cultural artifact, Graham shows that the fear and anxiety over technology's encroachment on the male rational subject works against an ethos of equity, diversity, and tolerance. For example, in *Star Trek: The Next Generation,* the android Lieutenant-Commander Data desires to act

42. Graham, *Representations of the Post/Human,* 226.

as and be understood as a human subject. In one episode his legal status as a free subject with rights is called into question when Commander Bruce Maddox wishes to experiment on him. He wins the trial and his capacity for self-determination by articulating the fact that his life is at stake.[43] In other episodes, Data longs for human emotion, but does not get it quite right, failing at poetry, stand-up comedy, and romantic relationships.[44] At the prospect of being dismantled, Data worries whether his digitized memories will contain the "essence" of the memory.[45] True humanity is marked out by what Data struggles to secure for himself, namely, liberty, emotive capabilities, and subjective experiences. Graham concludes that though *Star Trek* gives the appearance of attention to post/human difference, it defines authentic humanity as freedom and individuality by misrepresenting Data as an observer of human culture, always at the margins of full participation. As an ethos for constructing subjectivity, Graham observes, "This should encourage interpreters of representations of the post/human to be mindful of the invisibility or objectification—the misrepresentation—of those whose existence guarantees coherent categories, but whose non-participation or exclusion underpins the prosperity and security of others."[46] Following Derrida's observation that every seed of knowledge contains its own possible destruction, her analysis shows that attempts to describe an ontologically pure human nature subvert their own stable and fixed discourse by evoking alterity.

Third, we ought to consider an ethic of relationships in a theory of subjectivity. In particular, Graham argues that attending to "the digital, cybernetic and biotechnological" is cause to reflect on the porous peripheries between human and non-human. She uses the example of Donna Haraway's cyborg to show the contingency and hybridity of human nature. Human nature cannot be said to exist as it cannot be isolated from technology. With this in mind, a post/human ethic advocates attention to difference without dominion. Graham writes, "Ethically and experientially, the cyborg is a heuristic figure that suggests the rejection of solutions of either denial or mastery in favour of a post/human ethic grounded in complicity with, not mastery over, non-human nature, animals, and

---

43. Ibid., 138.
44. Ibid., 140.
45. Ibid., 139.
46. Ibid., 227.

machines."⁴⁷ Furthermore, the hybridity of human and technology leads to a co-evolution that is thoroughly material.

Lastly, when theorizing or analyzing subjectivity, we ought to reflect on deep motivations, especially fears and hopes. Graham does this well, observing that representations of the post/human contain a Gnosticism in their discourses of transcendence. The body and incorporality are denigrated while technology draws us toward the transcendent and spiritual. However, the idealism and dualism of the transcendence is "not so much about love of life, as paradoxically, a pathological fear of death, vulnerability, and finitude."⁴⁸ It is not the technophobic who is afraid of death, Graham argues, but the technophilic. From these insights, Graham concludes that the ideology of transcendence diminishes the sacramental nature of transcendence as embodied in person and technology. She observes, "This would acknowledge the fabricated, technologized world of human labour and artifice as equally capable of revealing the sacred as the innocence of 'nature.'"⁴⁹

Graham offers astute analysis of culture and the idea of the person. As one reviewer noted, this book reads like "an extended anthropological prolegomenon to a contemporary theology."⁵⁰ As a theory of subjectivity, she refrains from normative and teleological statements. Instead she unravels what informs our imagination to advocate for an enlarged ethic that refrains from turning the Other into a monster or alien. Her unique contribution is a turn to cultural studies and her analysis of the theological in everyday discourse. She does not write an explicit theological anthropology informed by feminist pastoral-practical theology,⁵¹ but, as I've shown, she does share rich insights that show how Others are made in discourse. How might her rich theological anthropology inform a praxis of just care that takes seriously identity?

47. Ibid., 229.
48. Ibid., 230.
49. Ibid., 233.
50. Elaine L. Graham, "Review of *Representations of the Post/Human*," 124.
51. I say pastoral-practical here because of Graham's context as a theologian in the United Kingdom. In the U.K. pastoral has tended to have a more expansive definition than in the U.S. Protestant contexts where pastoral often refers to the narrowed activities and research around care and counseling, while practical is the broader framework. See helpful definition entries on pastoral and practical theology in *Dictionary of Pastoral Care and Counseling* (1990).

## Subjectivity and the Social Self

Pastoral theologian Barbara J. McClure offers a theory of the social self, an individual who is the embodiment of social systems, contra "an asocial, ahistorical, 'authentic' self" who informs the practice and theories of pastoral theology, care, and counseling," in *Moving Beyond Individualism in Pastoral Care and Counseling*.[52] She argues that the individualistic paradigm is pervasively institutionalized in pastoral theology and its practices of care and counseling. She explains, "A liberal Protestant notion of selfhood—which provides the background for most of my training and prevails in most pastoral theology and practice—includes a generally optimistic focus on the individual's personal responsibility and ability to change, but does not account as well for the social and institutional realities that shape our experiences and our selves."[53] She argues that it is not enough for pastoral theology "to rail against" individualism or to "treat the negative effects."[54] Instead, pastoral theology must examine its "overly narrow conceptions of selfhood."[55]

McClure finds that a strong social construction theory accounts for the ways in which individuals are reflections of dominant systems, as well as how individuals are agents in these conditions. For McClure, a self encompasses all dimensions of the person—"thinking, feeling, acting, relating, giving, receiving, with conscious and unconscious elements, hidden and performative qualities, sinful, graced, alone and related, consistent and surprising."[56] The self is embodied, emotive, spiritual, and rational, and also much more, because the self is always embedded, reflective of, and in relationship with the social, and thus also power.

In this line of social theorizing, it is tempting to assume that a self dissipates under the oppressive tide of dominant systems, and thus becomes a deterministic theological anthropology. On the contrary, McClure asserts that a strong social theory shows how potent a synergistic view is in shaping a self's agency. She writes,

> When we fail to recognize the fact that we are ontologically synergistic selves who come into being in the dynamic interplay between our physical selves, our interpersonal relationships,

52. McClure, *Moving Beyond Individualism*, 200.
53. Ibid., 3.
54. Ibid., 5.
55. Ibid.
56. Ibid., 181.

and the sociocultural contexts in which we are all embedded, we fail to understand the importance of reflexive agency in the face of conditions that make for distressed, fragmented or depressed selves. The origin of our agency is in the interstices of social contexts that have constructed us, the contexts and experiences that have come together in unique ways, creating perspectives and forms of agency that are new.[57]

New perspectives and new forms of agency arise due to the thoroughly unique creation of that who is one's self. Each relationship with person, institution, and system and one's overall life experience contributes to the creation of a unique individual. Further, this is an ongoing, never-complete process.

Drawing from process and liberation theology, McClure develops a theology with strong normative visions for interpersonal relations between God, self, and others. Synergistic theology parallels the synergistic person. That is, God, like the self, is ever changing and responding to the actions of persons in the world; what does not change is the principle that God is love.[58] McClure writes, "God is immanent, related, and is constantly and in every moment doing everything within divine power to prevent and repair needless and destructive suffering. But God cannot act without the will, responsiveness, and creative engagement of persons who can participate in easing or even preventing suffering."[59]

The ramifications of a synergistic self, God, and society offer new opportunities to the field of pastoral theology, care, and counseling. A synergetic reality means that suffering is not an individual occurrence, but one connected to sociopolitical realities. Further, a synergetic reality presses upon our human agency and urges us to participate in the salvific work of changing oppressive institutions that uphold the status quo. This is the cultivation of the "kin-dom of God,"[60] and the work that must be done for the telos of human flourishing.

Following this theoretically rich material, McClure outlines theological, theoretical, practical, and organizational proposals for the field. She urges pastoral theologians to describe and effect the kin-dom of

57. Ibid., 201.

58. Ibid., 206.

59. Ibid., 208.

60. Ibid., 215. McClure cites mujerista theologian Ada Maria Isasi-Diaz's use of this term to describe the relatedness of persons as kin, brothers and sisters, and our participation in life together.

God, paying attention to who is able to access the institutions that support pastoral care and counseling. She argues that pastoral theologians must reclaim the capacity to name sin in order to make social critiques that lead to changes for better health. Theoretically, she urges pastoral theologians to move beyond individualism and develop "more socially adequate theological anthropologies."[61] Consequently, that which falls under the purview of pastoral theological praxis will continue to broaden into the public and social spheres.

What does this mean for the practice of pastoral care and counseling? First, pastoral caregivers and counselors must prioritize active engagement and participation rather than insight and withdrawal.[62] Second, the pastoral caregiver's physical office is a liminal space in which client and therapist must not only gain insight, but regain a sense of agency to change that which denigrates holistic flourishing. Third, pastoral caregivers must delineate the difference between the ideology of individualism and caring for an individual. Fourth, McClure writes that training will require an expansion of perspectives beyond ego psychology and one-on-one, long-term counseling. These implications will require organizational shifts, such as moving beyond the fee-for-service model and developing business models that build upon relationships between parishes and counselors.

McClure's call for more socially adequate theories of the self fund this project, as her work does not narrowly attend to the processes of intersubjective or social recognition. Without attending to these dynamics in her project, McClure does not account for how domination may disable a subject's ability to seek recognition as a step toward human flourishing. Furthermore, attending to recognition brings with it a consideration of the agency available to a socially constructed self. From a social construction perspective, a cultivation of agency through pastoral interaction ought to enable "resistance to relations of domination," while also acknowledging the constraints of agency that historical and social conditions make and maintain.[63] McClure's identification of the

61. Ibid., 240.

62. Ibid., 244.

63. Saba Mahmood, "Agency, Performativity, and the Feminist Subject," 180. As Mahmood shows in her description of the mosque movement, Egyptian Muslim women cultivate modesty or shyness as an expression of piety through embodied practices, such as wearing the hijab. While she argues these agentic practices shape "memory, desire, and intellect," her interpretation (and the women of the mosque

ideology of individualism at work in pastoral theology and praxis necessitates identification of other unexamined ideologies which construct our theological anthropology.

## Subjectivity and Multiplicity

Anglican priest, counselor, and feminist pastoral theologian Pamela Cooper-White provides an elegant theological description of the human person as multiple in her many essays and books. She is most explicit about her relational theological anthropology in *Many Voices: Pastoral Psychotherapy in Relational and Theological Perspective* (2007), though she wrestles complexly with questions of subjectivity, multiplicity, and the ethical dimensions of subject formation in a gathered collection of essays published under the title *Braided Selves: Collected Essays on Multiplicity, God, and Persons* (2011). In *Many Voices* she unfolds her nine characteristics of the human being that can be summed up in one sentence: "human beings are good, yet vulnerable; embodied; both alike and unique; intrinsically relational; multiple; mutable; loved, and therefore loving beings."[64] In articulating her description, Cooper-White provides the most systematic account of subjectivity as theological anthropology. Her feminist pastoral lens enables her to hold together paradoxes of the human condition.

A strong theology of God's presence acting in the world informs her first articulation that human beings are good and also vulnerable. A fundamental principle of Christian theology is the belief that God has acted and continues to act in the world—through creation, redemption in the life, death and resurrection of Jesus, and in the movement of the Holy Spirit. She concludes that there is goodness in all of creation because the triune God renews the face of the earth. Despite some Christian approaches to human sin that focus on total human depravity, she argues, "No matter how muddied and dim that spark of goodness may seem to the outside observer, however buried under layers of suffering, fear, and negative, even evil, behavior, this primordial goodness is the original

movement) is critiqued as participation in patriarchal systems of oppression rather than liberative feminist practice.

64. Cooper-White, *Many Voices*, 39.

inheritance of all created beings from the beginning of time."[65] A seed of goodness lies in the depth of all creation.

Second, Cooper-White states that human beings are embodied. She traces the Platonic separation of the body from the soul, and its use in early Christianity through the Reformation and Enlightenment, but then notes that the scriptures are "less dualistic."[66] She cites the linguistic unity for the words in the Hebrew Scriptures for body, soul, feeling, desire, and life, as well as Paul's emphasis on the body and soul as different orientations to the same whole person in the Christian Scriptures. With feminist and womanist theologians, she affirms the body as a location for knowledge of self and God.

Third, Cooper-White writes that human beings are both alike and unique. Drawing on the observation cited by pastoral theologian Emmanuel Lartey that every person is "like all others, like some others, and like no others,"[67] Cooper-White draws out conclusions that relate directly to subjectivity questions of identity, Otherness, justice, and recognition. Drawing on contemporary thinkers like Lévinas, Buber, Bhabha, and Spivak, Cooper-White theorizes the Other. An otherness always exists in our knowledge of other persons because each person is irreducible. She explains, "This emphasis in postmodernism and postcolonialism on restoring the speech and subjective stance of the 'other' has lifted up previously unheard and unseen individuals, and created a strong case for respect for the uniqueness of each human person and subgroup within larger society."[68] Yet, each other's demands for recognition raises challenges to our preconceived ideas of justice. Who are our neighbors? How are we to engage each other as our neighbors, especially when we may have competing demands?

Though every human may be like no other, we are also like some others. Cooper-White affirms that group identities are positive for human being: "Bonds of group and culture can create powerful communities and societies, knit together by ready empathy based on shared values and perceptions, and affection based largely on mutual identification."[69] However, she also warns that these bonds may also be negative, xenopho-

---

65. Ibid., 41.

66. Ibid., 42.

67. Lartey, *In Living Color*, 43.

68. Cooper-White, *Many Voices*, 45.

69. Ibid., 47.

bic, or exclusionary. Asserting a dialectical relationship between persons and culture, she emphasizes that new variations of culture and of persons in that culture arise as people go about the practice of their everyday life. Navigating the tension that we are like some others without falling into unknowable uniqueness of the individual, or claiming a removal of difference, is a significant ethical challenge.[70]

To be like all others is to affirm a shared sense of humanity that bolsters empathy and relationship amongst persons. However, Cooper-White also shows that an unconscious desire to deny difference and overemphasize sameness may be a developmental challenge where a person must cope with her internal differences. Drawing on cross-cultural research, she concludes that we are all alike in some aspects especially human affect and human needs, both of which are primary basis for assertion that all human beings are intrinsically relational.

We are relational by the fact that we live in communities, that we depend upon each other and creation for existence. "Humans live in *contexts*, which include both the natural environment and human-generated cultures," she writes.[71] Additionally the intrinsic relationality of the human person is God-given. She states "God uniquely created and bestowed human beings with the capacity for this relation, however obscured it may be by the brokenness of creation and the consuming preoccupations of daily human existence."[72] We long for deep connection with each other and with God.

So far, I have explained four features of Cooper-White's theological anthropology: that human beings are good and vulnerable; that human beings are embodied; that human beings are alike and unique; and that human beings are intrinsically relational. Cooper-White articulates four additional features: that human beings are multiple; that human beings are mutable, fluid, and in process; that human beings are loved; and that human beings are loving. I will flesh out the first two remaining features and briefly summarize the last two.

Weaving together relational psychology and postmodern French philosophy, Cooper-White deftly expands the idea of the person beyond a unitary self to a self of multiplicity. Additionally, she is attentive to the psychology that dialogues with pastoral theology, invoking Freud's

70. Ibid., 48.
71. Ibid., 51.
72. Ibid.

hydraulic model of the unconscious, preconscious, and conscious, as well as repression and drive theory, followed by object relations theory, to show a trajectory toward an expansive self. What is uniquely Cooper-White's is her use of French philosophers' Gilles Deleuze's and Félix Guattari's image of the rhizome to speak about the "multiply-constituted mind."[73]

In biological terms, rhizomes are root systems that spread out, moving horizontally, rather than rooting down vertically. Any person who has ever weeded to rid a landscape of bermuda grass understands the lessons of Deleuze's and Guattari's rhizomatic approach and their influence on Cooper-White's understanding of the mind as multiple: that a rhizome is connected at any point to anything; that it is heterogeneous, spreading out along networks that are not always visible or conscious; that the mind is spatially multiple, connected by lines, not points or nodes; that like an uprooted and ruptured rhizome, it can be torn from the ground, but will begin again, either starting from an old line or beginning a new one; that one's history must be mapped and remapped, not told in a genealogical fashion, particularly in light of getting at the roots of a pathology or neurosis; and lastly, that like the rhizome, there is no deep, predetermined structure, but instead "a form of mutable, open, experimental exploration."[74]

Cooper-White does not abandon psychoanalysis nor relational psychology and its emphasis on linking neuroses to events, behaviors, and feelings rooted in early childhood. Instead, she holds the psychoanalytic traditions in tension with the rhizomatic model. While psychoanalytic traditions would seek to find a singular, deep rooted cause, a rhizomatic model calls for "a different kind of associational chain of events—horizontal, at times more randomly selected, and linked by present conditions as well as past."[75] The result is a both-and approach that imagines the mind and subjectivity as both root and rhizome. Extending this metaphor, she describes the self as both tree and rhizome with branches that extend but continue to communicate:

> Imagine mind and self in terms of a three-dimensional multiplicity (or more)—neither vertical "depth" nor purely horizontal "plane," but an infinitely dimensional, quantum substance, with

73. Ibid., 58.

74. Ibid., 59

75. Ibid.

internal indeterminancy and some fluid external parameters. Imagine a subjectivity, a multiple self, identifiable as both an "I" and a "Thou" simultaneously, and with a mobile consciousness that scans and networks various parts of the "self," in an illusory but functional sense of self-cohesion, self-regulation, and self-continuity.[76]

In this understanding, there is no unitary self and no core self. The self is a being of "contingency and relatedness."[77] Cooper-White acknowledges that though this prospect might be frightening, it is also an opportunity to live creatively, exploring subjectivity, "Self," and "Others." Thus, Cooper-White argues that "human beings are mutable, fluid, and in process."[78]

As mutable, fluid, and in process subjects, heretofore unexplored dimensions of ethical and creative living beckon from the emancipation of living as a rational One. Rules, procedures, and individual rights are not the exclusive terrain for determining ethical behavior and just action. Instead, ethical and creative living is more like dancing, where each subject has space to move with funk, grace, and on or off the beat. Subjects may also mix multiple elements to make a new dance of freedom. It is bodily inhabitation with room "for those nonverbal mental contents that are only symbolic, or even presymbolic."[79] Yet, Cooper-White emphasizes that this new ethical and creative living comes with an expansion of conscience for oneself and for others, even as each continually grows, expands, and changes.

Finally, Cooper-White concludes that human beings are loved and loving beings. We are "profoundly known and loved by God,"[80] with our mutability, fluctuations, impermanence, and delicacy. Thus, human beings are also loving beings because the abundance of love for all creation spills across time and space. We are called to love each other—an ethic that calls us to "do justice, to love kindness, and to walk humbly with our God."[81]

Cooper-White's eight-fold theological articulation of the human person introduces a complexity to the subject that resonates with the complexity of modern experience. She brings the shifting terrains and

76. Ibid., 60.
77. Ibid., 62.
78. Ibid., 61.
79. Ibid., 63.
80. Ibid., 64.
81. Micah 6:8.

their viewpoints to pastoral theological anthropology with cogency and clarity while retaining a voice that affirms humans as *imago Dei* and challenges the fixity of this image, as well. In her later collection of essays, *Braided Selves*, Cooper-White explores multiplicity and difference in more depth. However, reflection on how to practice what a pastoral theological anthropology of multiplicity demands—in subject formation and in ethical action—deserves continued attention. For example, what events impede the formation of a multiple self? What happens when a subject is unable to scan and network various parts of the self to establish an illusory cohesion and continuity due to everyday injustices and oppressions?

In this chapter I argued that feminist pastoral theologians have been about the work of reflecting on the state of subjectivity both implicitly and explicitly by attending to the psychological and material effects of racism, classism, sexism, and heterosexism (Watkins Ali and Marshall), the representation of post/humans that is a refraction of what culture understands about the human condition (Graham), the social construction of the self (McClure), and theological anthropology for pastoral psychotherapy (Cooper-White). Their reflections are critical to continue to further refine descriptions of the subject. Feminist pastoral theologians Watkins Ali, Marshall, Graham, McClure and Cooper-White each offer a slice of the vision of the subject and her formation in light of theology, individual and relational psychology, and the sociopolitical and cultural difference. Common to all these views is concern for those who are marginalized, oppressed, or made other. I share these concerns, and as I reflected in Chapter One, I believe that theories of recognition contain insight for feminist pastoral theological constructions of subjectivity.

Along with Barbara J. McClure, I argue that a theory of psychological formation of the subject cannot be divorced from a social formation. To contribute to the discussions on subject formation from a psychological, social, and theological perspective, I dialogue with theories of recognition, concentrating on the feminist psychoanalyst Jessica Benjamin, feminist philosopher Judith Butler, and liberation theologian Marcella Althaus-Reid while also drawing on additional theorists and resources in the next three chapters. I argue that attending to the problem (and the solution) of recognition is necessary as we feminist pastoral theologians continue to explore how individuals and groups of persons become othered, how otherness is internalized, and also how resistance to oppressive systems of domination is to be cultivated for agency and transformation of self and society. Taking account of recognition from intersubjective, social, and theological perspectives enables feminist pastoral theologians to be on the look-out to develop critical accounts of persons whose voices are marginalized or disabled through misrecognition and non-recognition.

# 3

## Intersubjective Recognition

In the Gospel tradition of Mark, we hear Jesus' confusing and harsh words on discipleship: "If anyone comes to me without hating his father and mother, wife and children, brothers and sisters, and even his own life, he cannot be my disciple."[1] When I teach the course Personal Spirituality and Theology of Human Experience, students who have been engaged and curious become quiet or angry when I ask them how they understand Jesus' words. "That can't be in the Bible," is the most common response. Then they elaborate. "I was taught to love my family." "Family is everything." "You're nothing without family." Even students who later self-reveal and reckon with histories of familial abuse are taken abruptly by Jesus' words because they seem so at odds with what is observed as the primary locus of goodness, happiness, and sanctity found from all cultural sides. The family is supposed to be place of safety, growth, and love. Instead, many families consciously or unconsciously teach patterns of domination and submission. At the same time, families are the location where we first encounter another person and are given the opportunity to recognize them as a subject and not only an object. Encountering another person as a subject and not only an object is the process of intersubjective recognition. Intersubjective recognition is both primary good and task of family life, and especially of the first relationship between primary caretaker and child.

1. Luke 14:26.

As I've alluded, intersubjective recognition can be distorted beginning in family life and effectively create an environment where norms of intersubjective oppression inform social life. For example, a husband's right to beat his wife was cited as Common Law in the U.K. until the turn of the twentieth century, and continues as domestic violence today. A husband's domination over his wife continues to be cited as a theological precept, following from words attributed to Paul in Ephesians, "As the church is subordinate to Christ, so wives should be subordinate to their husbands in everything."[2] In the crudest of fashions, beating as domestic chastisement asserts patterns of male domination over women and fundamentally short circuits recognition. Intersubjective misrecognition and intersubjective non-recognition shape future experiences and patterns of personal suffering. On a large scale, these patterns of personal suffering shape patterns of social suffering, especially when reified through legal and theological spheres.

Domination and submission need not become the norm to achieve recognition. Intersubjective recognition can be mirrored between caretaker and child, and caretaker and other persons in the family, like partners, husbands, or wives, in loving, non-dominating ways. Intersubjective recognition as a developmental task paves the way for continued interactions as *circuits of recognition*, a phrase used by feminist psychoanalyst Jessica Benjamin to denote the iterative process of recognizing an other and being recognized by an other. Intersubjective recognition establishes the conditions for giving and receiving love, as well as emotional and spiritual growth.

This next chapter is dedicated to an exploration of intersubjective recognition, and particularly the problem of domination and submission, in dialogue with feminist psychoanalyst Jessica Benjamin. I argue that accounting for perspectives of intersubjective recognition in feminist pastoral theology and praxis provides opportunities to expand our conceptions of subjectivity, particularly through a lens attentive to gender, sexuality, justice, and care. First, I describe how intersubjective recognition is a formational and primary psychological task that begins in childhood in the context of family life. Second, I trace intersubjective recognition into adult relationships to examine how domination and submission as forms of relating are transmuted from sexual forms to social and political forms, shaping our subjectivity. Third, examining any

2. Ephesians 5:24.

relationship between mother and child must include critical comments about Freud's concept of the Oedipus complex. I offer an alternative reading of the Oedipus complex that accounts for gender as well as the problem of domination and submission following from Benjamin. Last, I consider additional critiques of Benjamin's work and offer introductory thoughts about the implications of her work to feminist pastoral theological constructions of subjectivity.

This chapter comes with a few warnings. First, it is tempting to think about the process of recognition as an either/or conundrum. Either, intersubjective recognition is achieved and two sovereign subjects may meet each other in mutual respect, both recognizing one another and asserting one to another, and thus establishing the basis for mutuality and love. Or, intersubjective recognition is not achieved and two subjects endlessly desire recognition, contorting themselves and their understanding of love to achieve recognition, but at great risk to loss of self. However, I would propose that intersubjective recognition is best understood through a spectrum approach. In any intimate relationship, there is always a spectrum between recognition and assertion as healthy bonds of love, and recognition and assertion that may move toward physical, sexual, and psychological domination and submission as destructive shackles that masquerade as love.

Second, while domination and submission as sexual practices both excite and stimulate, I am hesitant to argue that the only thing two persons must establish is a safe word and a set of rules. Through a critical feminist lens, the popularity of *50 Shades of Grey* by E.L. James and its sequels indicate the deep desire for intersubjective recognition, not domination and submission. I fear, however, that domination and submission is seen as one sexual choice among many and predominately from a heteronormative perspective: man on top or woman on top; man submissive or woman submissive. In truth, submission and domination creep up on us, making us subject to a set of unconscious propositions and beliefs that are acted out in relationship with another, whether teacher, parent, lover, child, or co-worker. What happens in the bedroom can become a set of norms of everyday social practice that denigrate the self-in-relation. It may be that submission and domination are possible in some relationship, but this choice must always be conscious and intentional. Psychological and spiritual maturity may be the very thing that enables safe surrender to another.

Finally, any discussion of domination and submission must account for the reality that modern day slavery takes the form of both sex trafficking and sex travel. Vulnerability, especially in minors, is a key factor in determining who is trafficked and coerced to participate in the sex trade. The Polaris Project, a non-profit named for the north star used by slaves along the Underground Railroad traveling to freedom, reports that pimps and sex traffickers control their victims through feigned affection, deception, violence, and threats.[3] For men and women, girls and boys, who find themselves in harmful situations of coercion and violence resulting from patterns of domination and submission, we describe and enact a praxis of recognition that aims for liberation, not submission.

## Intersubjective Recognition Begins at Home

Family, and particularly the relationship between child and primary caretaker (often, mother) is the starting point of intersubjective recognition and its distorted practice of domination and submission, notes Jessica Benjamin. Jessica Benjamin is a practicing psychoanalyst and adjunct faculty in New York University's Postdoctoral Program in Psychotherapy and Psychoanalysis. She is the author of *The Bonds of Love: Psychoanalysis, Feminism, and the Problem of Domination* (1988), *Shadow of the Other: Intersubjectivity and Gender in Psychoanalysis* (1997), and *Like Subjects, Love Objects: Essays on Recognition and Sexual Difference* (1998). Using a feminist lens, her work focuses on gender, social structures, intersubjectivity, and psychoanalytic theories such as object relations theory, relational psychology, and ego psychology. In *The Bonds of Love: Psychoanalysis, Feminism, and the Problem of Domination* Benjamin explores why we accept and perpetuate unequal relationships of domination and submission.

The heart of Benjamin's argument is centered around the tension between recognition and assertion and its gendered distortions in intrapsychic, familial, and social contexts. When women are not conferred recognition as subjects in their own right, they participate in the reproduction of gendered systems of domination in order to gain that which they seek: recognition. Instead of actually leading to recognition, women retain status as objects who cannot encounter an outside world. Advancing claims from sociologist Nancy J. Chodorow, Benjamin argues that

---

3. Polaris, "Sex Trafficking in the U.S.," lines 3–4, 13.

women are denied their subjectivity beginning in early childhood triangular relations between mother, daughter, and father, and reproduced through adulthood.[4] Women become receptive and domestic; men become active and worldly. Gender roles are internally detrimental for women and men as they recreate a patriarchal society in which women are dominated.

Drawing from and reconstructing psychoanalytic theory, Benjamin argues that domination and submission are complex psychological processes in which both parties participate. Domination and submission are part of an intersubjective process—one reproduced from childhood through adulthood, and with manifestations in family life, social institutions, and sexual relations. Domination and submission pivot on the psychological need and capacity for recognition as well as its response, assertion. The desire for recognition fuels domination. The need and desire for recognition is why a dominator comes to have power that results in submission of another. Because we desire to be recognized, subjects are willing to subject themselves to another's control in order to receive that very thing which we desire, namely recognition. Yet, receiving recognition in this manner requires "a breakdown of the necessary tension between self-assertion and mutual recognition that allows self and other to meet as sovereign equals."[5] In other words, as processes, intersubjective recognition, and domination and submission are built from the same needs and capacities of the human person—the same psychological stuff. However, they differ in how they ultimately constitute a subject in relationship with another subject: toward love in freedom, or the illusion of love, in shackles. However, the shackles of domination and submission can be transformed into circuits of assertion and recognition, particularly when we become aware of the affective dynamics of emotional congruency and libidinal object constancy. I explain these dynamics in conversation with Benjamin, beginning with a critique of Margaret Mahler's theory of human development.

In *The Psychological Birth of the Human Infant*, child psychiatrist Margaret Mahler and her coauthors argue that an infant develops

4. Chodorow, *The Reproduction of Mothering*, 208. Chodorow associates the reproduction of mothering with the reification of patriarchy. She writes, "Women's mothering, then, reproduces psychological self-definition and capacities appropriate to mothering in women, and curtails and inhibits these capacities and self-definition in men."

5. Benjamin, *The Bonds of Love*, 12.

through the separation-individuation process. Mahler writes that "separation consists of the child's emergence from a symbiotic fusion with the mother, and individuation consists of those achievements marking the child's assumption of his own individual characteristics."[6] Separation and individuation mark the emergence of a separate self, a self which is no longer fused, or in symbiosis, with the mother. In separation and individuation, the human infant comes understand himself as an I, and his mother as a not-I.[7] All this occurs within the first 24 months of the child's life. The ultimate goal of this process is libidinal object constancy. Libidinal object constancy is achieved through positive internalization of the mother figure. However, this cannot occur without a crisis.

Mahler argues that from 15–24 months the infant undergoes a rapprochement crisis. The toddler comes to understand that he and his mother are two separate persons. There is "an increased need, a wish for mother to share with him every one of his new skills and experiences, as well as a great need for the object's love."[8] Although the toddler wishes for symbiosis, his own increasing mobility and verbal communication become the tools which make evident to him that the symbiosis of his early months is impossible. The junior toddler "gradually realizes that his love objects (his parents) are separate individuals with their own personal interests. He must gradually and painfully give up the delusion of grandeur, often by way of dramatic fights with the mother . . ."[9] Through the rapprochement crisis the toddler begins to define his personality and attains a level of object constancy, namely by internalizing a positively cathected mother image, an image made possible through the development of trust between mother and child.[10]

Trust is a key component of the positive mother internalization. The toddler must have experienced safety and nurture as an infant in order to internalize a full representation of the mother object. A full representation of the mother requires that she not be split into either only good or only bad. The toddler may feel hate toward the object because she is not present to him. Yet, by internalizing the good aspects, he is able to self-soothe and call upon this inner representation of the mother. In doing

6. Mahler, Pine, and Bergman, *The Psychological Birth of the Human Infant*, 44.

7. Ibid.

8. Ibid., 77.

9. Ibid., 79.

10. Ibid., 110.

so, the toddler separates himself from the mother. Mahler concludes that separation of the self from mother is required in order to fully develop into a person with a unique personality and set of desires.

Benjamin critiques Mahler's theory for its emphasis on the separation of individuals as the only way to achieve a full and healthy personality. She argues, echoing psychoanalyst and infancy researcher Daniel Stern, that the infant is not born as a blank emotional and relational slate, unified to the mother out of necessity, who must then differentiate to become a person. Rather, the infant is a being who is interested in other persons from the very start. Benjamin explains, "Once we accept the idea that infants do not begin life as part of an undifferentiated unity, the issue is not only how we separate from oneness, but also how we connect to and recognize others; the issue is not how we become free of the other, but how we actively engage and make ourselves known in relationship to the other."[11]

Active engagement and making ourselves known shapes our formation as selves-in-relation. More importantly, being a self-in-relation shapes our capacity to be selves-in-community, a community that grows from our earliest and perhaps most important relationships with our primary caretakers. Against a Mahlerian approach, human development does not require a complete cut-off of self from others, especially objects of love and care. Instead, I become myself more fully by being in relationships in which assertion and recognition are balanced. This intersubjective perspective describes a new norm of human development based on relationality and critiques an exclusively intrapsychic perspective.

A circuit of assertion and recognition is at the heart of human development from an intersubjective perspective. Benjamin writes, "A person comes to feel that 'I am the doer who does, I am the author of my acts,' by being with another person who recognizes her acts, her feelings, her intentions, her existence, her independence. Recognition is the essential response, the constant companion of assertion."[12] A subject declares "I am, I do" and receives the response "You are, You have done."[13] These kinds of reflexive moments build on each other. As a young self asserts herself through action, she is recognized by the other who can mirror the

11. Benjamin, *The Bonds of Love*, 18.

12. Ibid., 21.

13. Ibid.

emotions displayed through the action. Each act of assertion followed by recognition serves to build a positive sense of a self-in-relation.

Circuits of recognition and assertion may be verbal, but are also communicated through emotions. Emotional congruence between two persons affirms that recognition is indeed happening, and leads to feelings of connection, rather than feelings of separation. Benjamin gives the example of a child shaking a rattle in joy. The mother shows that she feels similarly happy "by matching his level of intensity in a different mode (she whoops)."[14] While the child is happy with the rattle, the mother is happy because her child is happy, and so they share similar emotions despite a difference in causation. The shared emotions between mother and child are part of the emotional attunement of the two subjects. The pleasure of the child produces pleasure in the mother who in turn shows that same pleasure to the child. In doing so, the mother recognizes her child as a self capable of impacting others. Developmentally, each act of recognition builds toward a self capable of emotional congruency. Learning emotional congruency aids in the development of an empathic self-in-relation.

This intersubjective perspective positively affirms the relational process of becoming oneself, but also brings challenges to development and maturation. If we take as a starting point the intersubjective claim that I must look outside myself to receive recognition, an iterative process which ideally affirms my sense of agency and responsibility, then it follows that my development of self is dependent upon another. Intersubjective recognition may follow an assertion of self; intersubjective recognition may not follow an assertion of self. To be clear, one or two discrete failures to recognize do not imperil long term human development.

However, an internalized self-other conflict can arise which places the meeting of sovereign selves in jeopardy. Benjamin argues that a one year old infant can feel the conflict between internally desiring something, like wanting to turn a light switch on and off, and her parents' desire for the lights to remain either off or on. The infant's desire to remain emotionally attuned to her parents, despite her internal wishes, can be transmuted into submission to her parents' will, or as she grows, another's will.[15] Thus, as the child asserts herself, internal conflict arises from the need for recognition. At psychological best, the child becomes the

14. Ibid., 30.
15. Ibid., 31.

adult who asserts and "experiences his own agency and the distinctness of the other," even when recognition in the form of tacit approval does not come.[16] But this is not always the case, as we see when we examine submission and domination in adult sexual relationships.

## Domination and Submission as Extremes of Recognition

"Both this flogging and the chain attached to the ring of your collar . . . are intended less to make you suffer, scream, or shed tears than to make you feel, *through* this suffering, that you are not free but fettered, and to teach you that you are totally dedicated to something outside yourself," writes Pauline Réage, author of *The Story of O*, a tale of erotic submission of a woman to her sexual male master.[17] Jessica Benjamin uses this story to show how an unfulfilled desire for recognition transmutes into a desire for fusion. Fusion and merger create submission; submission is accompanied by a loss of subjectivity. Paradoxically, submission results in the fulfillment of the desire to be recognized. From this story Benjamin considers how "domination is anchored in the hearts of those who submit to it."[18] In this next section, I explain how domination and submission are powerful psychological motivations in sexual relationships that lead to relational distortions between two selves.

Situated as one chapter ("Master and Slave") within her text, Benjamin's interpretive reading of *The Story of O* is an illustration of the extremes of domination and submission. Using this provocative story, which I briefly narrate below, Benjamin gives a concrete, but *extreme*, example of the psychological destruction of woman as "other" and "object" through denial of recognition. She describes the female submissive, O, as a subject who attaches herself to a masculine idealized authority figure. The idealized authority figure represents a father figure who liberates her from an engulfing mother figure. By identifying with the idealized father figure, submissive women hope to gain freedom rather than repeat their mother's experience. That is, seeing the mother dominated within sexist and misogynistic family and social relations, and yet being dependent upon her, the daughter moves towards a figure who can free her from the bondage of becoming an other and an object. Benjamin explains, "The

16. Ibid.
17. Réage, *The Story of O*, 17.
18. Benjamin, *The Bonds of Love*, 52.

denial of subjectivity to women means that the privilege and power of agency fall to the father, who enters the stage as the first outsider, and so represents the principle of freedom as denial of dependency."[19] Paradoxically, movement toward and identification with the idealized figure does not guarantee freedom, but reproduces submission.

The problem of submission is even more complex because interpersonal occasions of submission and domination are socially reproduced. Viewing one's mother as object creates a normative pathway to view women as objects in society at large. Benjamin writes, "Only a mother who feels entitled to be a person in her own right can ever be seen as such by her child, and only such a mother can appreciate and set limits to the inevitable aggression and anxiety that accompany a child's growing independence."[20] Yet what results in mother/woman as object and father/ man as subject is a gendered split, what Benjamin calls gender polarity. Gender polarity pervades "social relations, our ways of knowing, our efforts to transform and control the world."[21] Confronting and unraveling the effects of gender polarity requires that we disentangle the intersubjective ties of domination and submission so that they become circuits of recognition and assertion. It is from within this context and hope that Benjamin gives us the portrait of O as a severe case study of warped and distorted recognition.

Circuits of recognition and assertion gone awry become chains of domination and submission. Like recognition and assertion, the chains of domination and submission are forged through an intersubjective process. Thus, the circuit of domination and submission is not oppositional to recognition, but made possible by the desire for recognition and assertion. Domination "is the twisting of the bonds of love."[22] Rather than repress the desire for recognition, domination "enlists and transforms it."[23] From a theological perspective, the sin of domination is a trick. It makes use of what we most desire, what we most want for ourselves, and which can only be received from the hands of another. When the necessary tension between self and other dissipates, the dominated person

19. Ibid., 221.

20. Ibid., 82.

21. Ibid., 220.

22. Ibid, 219.

23. Ibid.

allies herself to others "who personify the *fantasy* of omnipotence."[24] The fantasy resides where another/an Other should exist.

It is important to note that domination-submission as a warped process of recognition is a serious game of subjective agency. Submission and domination are agential psychic forces that are tied together from the very start. Paradoxically, both parties desire recognition even when their actions would drive them further away from a truly mutual exchange of assertion and recognition. A lack of mutuality in recognition is not one-sided. Both agents are involved and both submit to and dominate each other, though in distinct ways. However, because seeking recognition may be an unconscious process, an empathic stance allows us to interpret this extreme means as search and desire for love, and not merely as a binary story of victimization and blame.

In *The Story of O*, a female fashion photographer, O, submits to eroticized branding, chaining, whipping, masking, blindfolding, and piercing. She is trained to be available at any time for anal, oral, and vaginal intercourse. Yet, she is also asked to give her consent to her own torture. As the story begins, O is brought to the château at Roissy by her lover, René. She is trained to serve the group of men who gather at Roissy, including René. After her initial training, René places her in the hands of a more dominant master, Sir Stephen, as an act of love, trust, and generosity to O. Her continued domination is generous as her pleasure is dependent upon being dominated by another. Under the tutelage of Sir Stephen, O masters her role as submissive, agreeing to a labia piercing and a branding of Sir Stephen's initials and insignia. At the climax of the story, O appears completely naked at a public party, save for an owl-like mask. She is treated solely as an object. The message of the story is clear: O is now an animal who has abandoned her own freedom.

*The Story of O* is not merely a tale of submission, but teaches us about the nature of violence, coercion, and chains of misrecognition and non-recognition in three ways. First, it shows how submission for the gain of recognition is enticing. Second, it demonstrates the pain and suffering that individuals will undergo in order to achieve recognition and that masquerades as love and acceptance. Lastly, it teaches us about the entanglement between the psyches of dominated and dominator.

Talk of domination and submission often engender feminist theological, political, and social disgust because we assume that there is

24. Ibid.

nothing to be gained by submission. This is a falsehood. Indeed, there is much to be gained through submission, including pleasure, recognition, and a certain kind of security, even if it is one where pathogenic beliefs constitute reality and recreate pathogenic beliefs into life action again and again. Human development is so deeply tied to recognition that even its most twisted versions evoke and fill the psychological needs normally associated with a non-sadomasochistic love relationship between self and other.

Patterns of domination and submission are transmitted from generation to generation in families. To achieve independence, a child must receive recognition from those she has been dependent upon. In families where the mother/primary caretaker and child are undifferenti- ated, patterns of domination and submission occur. Take, for example, the mother who is unsatisfied with her life and lives out her life through her child. The child comes to identify with the mother, not out of desire, but out of psychic necessity. The child receives a form of approval—often mistaken as love and acceptance—when she fulfills the mother's desires. Her submission to her mother's desires fulfills her need for intersubjec- tive recognition while at the same time suppressing her capabilities for self-determination.

For the child who is only recognized for what she can provide to the mother-figure, recognition and its fruits of independence and decision- making are suppressed. The child feels abandoned because she is unable to exact the kind of emotive outpouring that accompanies recognition by the primary caretaker. It is not that the child stops asserting her existence with the expectation of recognition. Rather, the hole left by a lack of rec- ognition, which in healthy maturation the adult self ought to be able to fill intrapsychically, is filled by relationships to patterns and things (like addictions and unhealthy relationships) which mirror the twisted prima- ry bond of love. Thus, the same pattern repeats itself with lovers, friends, therapists, strangers, and even institutions, resulting in relationships of submission and domination. These patterns are formed by pathogenic beliefs about the self in relation to others. Even more importantly, the drive behind the pattern is one's psychic safety, albeit safety is twisted to mean lack of mutuality and vulnerability in relationship to the other.

*The Story of O* exemplifies how the bonds of twisted love developed in psychic relationship to primary caretakers can occur in eroticized physical relationships. Instead of the psychic pain of failed recognition, O submits to physical pain. Benjamin writes,

> The pain of violation serves to protect the self by substituting physical pain for the psychic pain of loss and abandonment. In being hurt by the other, O feels she is being reached, she is able to experience another living person. O's pleasure, so to speak, lies in her sense of her own survival and her connection to her powerful lover. Thus as long as O can transpose her fear of loss into submission, as long as she remains the object and manifestation of his power, she is safe.[25]

Perhaps safety was unavailable to her as a child, and so as an adult, O takes refuge in her dominator, Sir Stephen. His domination is her protection.

Through her submission, O gains the same kind of recognition that she desires. It is a recognition in which physical pain substitutes for psychic pain. Recognition is made possible by her submission to a master to whom she can bind her desire to his will. Yet, O does not feel her submission as pain. Instead, it is pleasurable. In the text, O shows off her scars to her friend Jacqueline. They are a source of pleasure and a source of pride to her, even though Jacqueline is disgusted. O's pained pleasure is secondary only to her master's pleasure, and in fact is dependent upon her ability to take refuge in a more dominant power, that of her master. Freud identified pain as a reaction to a stimulus that the body or ego cannot endure. When the body or ego can no longer endure, we submit to pain. Pleasure, on the other hand, responds and masters a stimulus. As Freud suggested, pain become pleasure creates conditions for mastery. However, it is only the master who experiences pleasure, not the submissive because the experience of pain is not an illusion. Thus, O experiences pain, not pleasure. Benjamin writes,

> O's loss of self is *his* gain, O's pain is *his* pleasure. For the slave, intense pain causes the violent rupture of the self, a profound experience of fragmentation and chaos. It's true that O now welcomes this loss of self-coherence, but only under a specific condition: that her sacrifice actually creates the master's power, produces his coherent self, in which she can take refuge.[26]

By her submission, O gains a freedom that she believes she never would have been able to access on her own. The power of submission lies in psychically understanding that O's psyche merges with one greater than herself. She believes that she gains, even if she is lost and destroyed in

25. Ibid., 61.
26. Ibid.

the process. Her gain in relinquishing control is mastery of anxiety. She is no longer in charge of decision-making or self-determining, and thus no longer anxiously seeks recognition from another. She has fused herself to another.

In intersubjective processes of recognition, the submissive is not the only person to suffer. Masters suffer as well, but from withheld consent and withheld pain infliction, rather than reception. For the master, pleasure is derived not only in the acts of domination, but also through the responsiveness and consent of the slave. Every question of consent posed by the master contains within it the potential for refusal by the slave, and thus ratchets up the power-laden tension between the two. In each act of bearing pain, the master derives pleasure. He gives pain to another in order to experience pleasure. Giving pain fulfills his desire for dominance. As such, the submissive holds the key to the master's pleasure and so pleasure is derived from the fulfillment of his desire to be dominant. Withheld fulfillment to be dominant, that is, refusal on the part of the Submissive to be submissive, is another steel link in the intersubjective shackles that bar circuits of mutuality. In a more colloquial way, the phrase "the bottom is in charge" speaks to this element. Thus, in another circular twisting of the chains of domination-submission, the master suffers when the slave does not consent to recognize his assertion of domination. His desire to be a master is his Achilles heel.

While Benjamin answers the question of why the dominated submit, she does not explicate the value of sexual domination-submission. In the essay, "This grass is very dark to be from the white heads of old mothers," Michael Joseph Gross recounts his experiences attending the annual International Mister Leather, the largest convention of leather men in the world and a gathering filled with masters and slaves, "Daddies" and "boys." Gross tells us why sexual submission and domination are powerful intersubjective tools. He shows us the currencies at work in these relationships—currencies of shame, power, abandonment, pleasure, and even beauty—which increase in value over time. The shackles are strong because they are valued in the socially constructed world.

Contrary to Benjamin's reading of O in which submission results in loss of power and subjectivity, and makes a subject into an object, Gross argues that there can be good submission, even playful submission, where sovereignty of subjects is retained by developing a contract of conduct hinging on a safe word. He writes,

The good Daddies I have known have had one thing in common: they use humiliation to paradoxical effect, revealing how absurd shame actually is. Daddy calls boy his bitch; he brings the bottom's hidden shame into the open and plays with it, makes shame a source of pleasure, beauty, and even power. The first leather top I met taught me a maxim of the leather world—that the bottom is always in control, because the bottom chooses a safe word at the beginning of the scene. A good top knows how to read his bottom, to take him to his limits of pleasure or pain, and then push just beyond it. For the times when Daddy's judgment fails, however, the safe word is the bottom's power. I say that word, the scene is done.[27]

In this account, the potential effects of good submission are intrapsychic growth through intersubjectivity. Safe words establish the boundaries of a scene in which each subject acts in the interest of the other and oneself. Like the healthy bonds of love, submission-domination as described by Gross can be circuitous: a subject desires to assert himself and be recognized by another, another subject desires to be receptive to assertions and to recognize another. In this circuit of good submission, which has the potential to go terribly wrong, the currency of shame—that is, desiring to be submissive, desiring to be dominant—is converted into currencies of pleasure, beauty, and sovereign power. It behoves us to ask whether this is a real illusion. By real, I mean to imply that the experience is true, occurring, experienced, remembered. By illusion, I point toward the caughtness of submission and domination. That is, can intersubjectively forged chains of domination and submission actually fulfill the telos of the very desires it enlists and then shackles?

Gross reveals that there is deep psychology at work in the sadomasochistic relationship where a submissive's power to continue or end a scene—or relationship—values over time. It is an emotional currency that illustrates why being a master is tempting: binding another to oneself relieves the existential fear of abandonment. Gross relays another conversation he had with a Daddy named Tony: "He told me that his last relationship had been a three-year Master/slave arrangement. He said that he had thought that being a Master was the ultimate safeguard against being abandoned. 'I thought if I owned him, he would never leave me.'"[28] Contrary to what the externals look like in a sadomasochistic

27. Gross, "The grass is very dark," 156.
28. Ibid., 157.

relationship—Tony as master dominating or producing pain in another for his own pleasure—the internal power dynamic is the opposite. Tony is not innately cruel with no emotion; rather, Tony is filled with emotions. Self-aware, he remorsefully indicates that he never wanted to be abandoned.

How does the line between reality and play mark peripheries in a praxis of intersubjective recognition? Here again the real illusion of domination-submission provides us with a conceptual framework to read the reflections of a dominant that Gross interviewed. Gross writes,

> When I asked one sexy, single Master whether he and his slave would ever break character when they were in public, he said, "I don't think of these as roles. This is who we are. Most people in our lives would not know that we are Master and slave. But I would dominate him in subtle ways in public. He would open the door for me as we enter a restaurant. When I realized that I'd forgotten my glasses in the car, he would retrieve them."[29]

Fetching another's reading glasses and opening the door for another are rather mundane activities. They are not ones we might associate with domination, but instead with courtesy or even love. That the master can seemingly dominate his servant in these most pedestrian activities shows us the real illusion of the chains, twisted tightly, like a noose, cutting off the flow of assertion-recognition, but which we come to believe are enlivening. We are made to believe that this is love at its best. Yet, as Sir Stephen so clearly reminds O, "You're confusing love and obedience. You'll obey me without loving me, and without my loving you."[30] In reality, Sir Stephen's words are fiction. Rarely is the loss of freedom and self-determination so adeptly and straightforwardly conveyed or perceived.

## Correcting Father, and Freud

The problem of domination and submission is not just pillow talk. It is a problem with patterns that recircuit and shackle people across the ecological spectrum of social institutions. Domination and submission is specifically reiterated between the sexes in a phenomena that Jessica Benjamin identifies as gender polarity. To understand the phenomena, Benjamin critically examines the Oedipal complex and considers how

29. Ibid.

30. Réage, *The Story of O*, 86.

it normalizes women's roles as emotive engulfers while men are made as autonomous and rational selves. Both roles are internalized, externalized, and reified. As a critique and corrective to Freudian-shaped psychoanalytic psychology, Benjamin argues that what was assumed to be normative—Freud's Oedipus complex—is actually sexist ideology posturing as normal human behavior. The patriarchal, sexist result is the norm of women as receptive, done-to, and objects, while men are active, doers, and subjects.

Freud developed the Oedipus complex as part of his psychosexual theory of development. Named after character Oedipus Rex, who accidently kills his father and marries his mother in Sophocle's drama, the Oedipus complex describes how a boy resolves his longing for his mother and his jealousy of his father. During the phallic stage of development from ages three to five, a boy desires his mother, and wants to possess her. He is jealous and angry of his rival—his father. To resolve the Oedipal complex and become a healthy adult, the boy must identify with his father. While the boy's id wants to kills the father, the ego knows that the father is stronger than the boy and fears castration. Castration anxiety, fear of literal and figurative emasculation, is reinforced when the boy looks at his mother and sees that she is weaker than his father and without a penis. He assumes that she has been punished and had her penis removed. Wishing to avoid castration, the boy must identify with his father and cease desire of his mother. His rational ego suppresses his animalistic id urges to kill his father and takes his mother. The resolution of this complex leads to an internalization of the father figure in the form of the super-ego, an idealistic moral authority within the self that polices the urges of the id and makes the ego act in accordance with the super-ego's idealism.

Critiquing Freud, Benjamin argues that the Oedipus conflict is the locus for gender polarity and is problematic. The Oedipus complex is not the norm of healthy development. Instead, she argues that gender polarity leads to splitting, which is an unhealthy attempt by the self to categorize a subject or object into categories of all good or all bad. Splitting is either/or thinking. When splits occur, such as in the Oedipal complex, a boy is groomed from childhood to see all good and all bad through the lens of gender. His mother is all bad and his father is all good. Women are all bad and are penalized through subjugation for disobeying father, and men are all good and powerful, ensuring order and taming women in interpersonal relationships, families, and the world. Benjamin does not deny the theory of the Oedipus complex, but interprets it through a lens attentive to harmful gender polarity.

Like her critique of Mahler, Benjamin argues that Freud's description of the Oedipal conflict is based on the false assumption that individuation requires absolute separation for the creation of an autonomous, psychologically healthy self. Boys are made to repudiate all of that which is feminine in order to become men. Fathers serve a primary role in forcing the choice. The boy can be coddled by the mother and remain in the domestic sphere or the boy can choose to become an autonomous agent and access the public sphere. Identification with the mother is "a seductive threat to autonomy."[31] While the boy may desire his mother's nurture and protection, he realizes that she is weak and subjugated by the father. If the boy identifies with the mother, he will not be protected and nurtured. Male individuation thus requires a hard and sound split from the mother. To control his desire for the maternal even while repudiating it, the man-boy psychically separates himself from any feminine attributes contained within. What cannot exist within himself also cannot exist within family or political life. As the autonomous male subject is created, the female becomes a non-subject. Males are subjects with autonomy and agency; women are objects.[32]

The result of the split is an idealization of the maternal and feminine while at the same time repudiating it from the male perspective. The feminine then becomes a fantasy that the male subject can project onto the female object. As a result, she retains an omnipotent status within the male psyche without the male ever having to be presented with the dissolution of her omnipotence as a real person who feels, emotes, fails, asserts, and recognizes. In short, she can remain perfect because she is an object who can be dominated in the male fantasy. With no agency, the male idealization of the fantastic maternal is never challenged.[33]

Male rationality requires that the emotional reasoning associated with the feminine be cut off. In this way, the autonomous individual is a non-feeling individual whose wants, needs, and desires have nothing to do with emotions. The autonomous male must cut himself off from all that would threaten his ability to be absolute and independent, and so he (and society) creates an idealized mother who will never threaten

31. Benjamin, *The Bonds of Love*, 136.
32. Ibid.
33. Ibid., 214.

him. The creation of the idealized mother is the ultimate psychological paradox, though. For in attempting to cut himself off from the real or introjected mother figure, he threatens his own sense of self-coherence as rational agent. He desires her unconsciously even while consciously pushing her and all that she stands for further away. This internal self-destruction is played out in family and social life. And there is no winner in this battle. Benjamin writes, "The self's aspiration to be absolute destroys the self, as well as the other, for as long as the other cannot face the self as an equal in the struggle, the battle results in loss, and not mutual recognition."[34]

Erotic submission is an evocative example of male domination, but theological discourse around it focuses primarily on the morality of sexual positions. Likewise, domestic violence is an overt example of domination, but distracts us from considering how submission and domination are engendered in more subtle ways through social institutions and practices. What continues to be needed is a critique of mundane male domination that inculcates belief in the naturalness of the autonomous individual, instrumental reason, and accumulation of wealth. As Benjamin observes, "It is this protean impersonality that makes it so elusive."[35] Male rationality is both pervasive and destructive. It distorts the recognition process in society and "eliminates the maternal aspects of recognition (nurturance and empathy) from our collective values, actions, and institutions" while also reducing assertion, social authorship, and agency.[36] It is insidious, but not irreparable. Here is the clarion call for recognition beginning as an intersubjective practice. Shackles must become circuits. Recognition between equal subjects can occur, but only by sustaining the paradoxical tension between assertion and recognition. While we have simultaneous needs for both recognition and for independence, the other who is required for our recognition is the very same other who can cripple our independence.[37] Thus, according to Benjamin, we must embrace this paradox to begin to undo the bonds that would bind. This is an ongoing, imperfect process, but one to which we must aspire, accepting "the inevitable inconstancy and imperfection of our efforts, without relinquishing the project."[38] By acknowledging the

34. Ibid., 215.
35. Ibid., 216.
36. Ibid., 218.
37. Ibid., 221.
38. Ibid., 224.

inconstancy and imperfection of our efforts to recognize each other, we become agents who can identify where the tension has broken down. When we can see where tension has led to collapse, we can create the space between subjects that would restore tension. If we refuse to do so, not only will our personal desires for recognition be unfulfilled, but so will our hopes for social transformation.

## Critiques and Implications for Feminist Pastoral Theology

As a theory of subjectivity, Benjamin has much to offer. First, she provides an etiology of domination and submission by tracing child development in relationship to primary caretakers, a dynamic which also finds its way into the bonds of love between partners. Second, she names patriarchy and its ensuing dynamics of submission and domination as problematic and also indicts the reproduction of patriarchy from generation to generation through family systems. Third, she critiques psychoanalytic psychology, explaining that what was assumed to be normative—Freud's Oedipus Complex—is actually sexist ideology posturing as normal human behavior. Fourth, she gives agency to men and women, arguing that to counteract patriarchy both genders must make the difference to balance the uneven scales from submission/feminity and domination/masculinity to mutual recognition/assertion. Lastly, Benjamin does not shy away from images and themes of the body, sex, and desire. She is explicit and graphic, a deviation from feminist theorizing that sterilizes sexuality. Essayist Phyllis Grosskurth comments, "She is concerned with the strong puritanical streak among feminists and its consequences. In their attacks on pornography and campaigns for its censorship, some seem to have rejected sex, its fantasies, and its pleasures altogether."[39] Benjamin challenges her readers to refuse to gloss over the erotic.

How might Benjamin's insights be useful to constructing subjectivity attentive to, but not hampered by, identity in feminist pastoral theology? Recall the case I described in Chapter 1 of women seeking ritualized care after child loss. I was perplexed by the presentations of the women who suffered. In my interviews with chaplains I had expected to hear about how specific personal and social identities shaped the experience of suffering the loss of a child, but did not. At the same time, I juxtaposed this evidence against the written record of feminist pastoral theology

39. Grosskurth, "The New Psychology of Women," 31.

which has produced a significant amount of literature that speaks to identity and pastoral care. In order to better attend to persons in our caring and writing practices, our identity paradigm must be in conversation with theories of recognition, as they help us to understand how oppression and domination as forms of social suffering manifest in individual lives. Benjamin illuminates how suffering is weaved into the textures of everyday existence, particularly in forms of domination and submission in personal relationships. In regard to the women seeking care, we ought to examine the caregiving relationship for patterns of harm, especially patterns of domination-submission as well as gender polarity couched in theological precepts. Were the women recognized in their subjectivity? Were they capable of asserting themselves? Additionally, many of the women also experienced poverty. As such, pastoral theologians must also question if the women experienced barriers to prenatal care. Doing so links concerns about health justice to feminist pastoral theology's imperative to describe and enact praxes for human flourishing.

Benjamin has done us a great service by showing how recognition is a fundamental human desire, and as such, the extent to which we will go to receive recognition—extents which include severe physical pain, and human degradation until we become, and become to believe, that we are objects meant solely for the use by another. The loss of self to another in order to have self-worth affirmed is tragic. Further, the one who receives the lost self of submission and capitalizes on the need to be affirmed by wielding domination as power is also a tragedy. Yet, Benjamin remains hopeful that the balance can be found. With enough self-knowledge and enough self-will the destructive patterns of domination and submission can be rooted out. Individual men will recognize individual women and say the words that we all long to hear: "I love you. You are awesome and amazing." Individual women (and men) will assert themselves to each other: "I love me. I am awesome and amazing." It is assumed that from these words right action and right treatment worthy of all human dignity will flow. Psychic splits can be reunited; gender polarity can be reversed.

I am hopeful that psychic splits can be reunited and gender polarity reversed, but it is a measured hope given the constraints of the assertion-recognition circuits. When a subject is malformed and does not possess the capability to assert oneself in sexual or psychological relationships, theorists of subjectivity must be careful not to mistake coerced consent for conscious or unconscious submission. Benjamin's reflections fail to take into account surrenders that are neither sexual nor psychological, but socially and politically coerced through political systems that do bodily violence. These kinds of surrenders are the injustices of victims who have no choice, but give "consent" under extreme duress from overwhelming and coercive exercises of power.[40] Submission is forced. If one concludes from Benjamin's theory that all subjects have the power to say no, the unintended result is the formation of a subject-agent who may be blamed for his or her lot in life, without examination of the systems or networks that surround that person.

There are circumstances when no "safe" word is available and when assertion requires that one end a relationship. Cycles of interpersonal violence, like domestic abuse and battering, are topics which pastoral theologians have brought to the church for reflection and action that fall into this category.[41] However, there are cycles of violence where one does not wish to participate but must because there is no personal exit strategy. Furthermore, it may be the case that assertion at the socio-political level leads to death, especially in the case of political repression where asylum is not granted. For feminist pastoral theology, accounting for intersubjective recognition is a first step. In addition to analyzing the circuits of domination and submission at the intersubjective level of subject formation, theological reflection on subjectivity must also account for the violence of domination and submission at the social-political level and it effects on the individual. Attending to social and political violence helps us to analyze the effects of social suffering at the individual level.

In this chapter I presented Jessica Benjamin's psychological theory of recognition and assertion. I described how an imbalance in the bonds of love can morph the circuits of recognition to chains of submission and domination. I argued that her theory provides a crucial grounding point for feminist pastoral theologians to reflect on the role of recognition in subject formation. I briefly critiqued her theory for relying too heavily on an assent to submission and a capability to mutually engage in the process of assertion and recognition, themes I explore in Chapter 7. In the next chapter, I examine the importance of social recognition to marginalized selves- and communities-in-relation in dialogue with the work of Judith Butler. At its best, social recognition is a key feature to correct

40. Person, "Why It's So Sweet to Surrender," lines 58–60. I echo Person's critique that Benjamin's "major omission is her failure to distinguish psychological surrender, whether to love, mysticism, or religion, from the necessary submission to overpowering force – a pure victimhood."

41. See Adams, *Woman Battering*; and Cooper-White, *Cry of Tamar*.

injustices and advance emancipatory possibilities. However, when selves and communities are misrecognized or not recognized at all, the capability for growth, liberation, and self- and communal-determination are not only repressed, but also may become matters of life and death.

# 4

## *Social Recognition*

As I scan through my bookshelf, I can see clearly the shape of the field of feminist pastoral theology, care, and counseling. Titles such as *Counseling Women, Women Out of Order, Women in Travail and Transition,* and *Counseling Lesbian Partners* are visible. Drawing from second wave feminist commitments, the field has paid particular attention to the experiences of women, and then opened the way for inclusion of women whose intersecting identities call us to further reflection on our practices of caring.[1] As I paged through several of these texts, I found a question for self-reflection interspersed between notes inside the front cover reflective of this paradigm: "What social identity groups do I belong to?" Asking this question through the prism of recognition, care, and justice prompts many more: Which social-political identity matters the most? How does living my identities promote equality and justice? Do my identities actually describe who I am and who I want to become? What are the contributions that I bring to feminist pastoral theology through the identities I inhabit and the experiences that have shaped me?

My first answers to the question I posed myself reveal the tension I feel in the use of identity in advancing a care that does justice. Identity politics, which has informed social justice inquiry and action since the

---

1. See Lassiter, "No Easy Resolution," for a thorough review and analysis of feminist pastoral literature which I argue utilizes an identity framework to organize caring responses.

1960s in the United States, did not fit how I understood myself because of the inadequacy of any single identity marker to represent my embodied experiences. I was the confluence of all these things; I could not choose one that was most authentic. At the same time, I worried that I did not measure up to any of the identities that I inhabit, and which inhabit me. Will social recognition be conferred upon me?

Women experience social suffering by who they are and what identities they occupy. It is vital that we understand identity as a crucial element in the formation of one's subjectivity. Although recognition proceeds through relationships between persons, social institutions, and cultural and political regimes, it is mediated through identity. As well, identity is formed in relationship to persons, social institutions, and cultural and political regimes who confer or deny recognition. While identity is not the whole and sum of a person, it is an aspect of a much fuller subjectivity that emerges in a future horizon. Still, identity is a means by which we evaluate whether a subject is like us or not like us in a present moment. Identity is also one means through which we seek recognition. We identify people who are like us in gender, race, sexuality, or ability in order to organize and advocate for ourselves. Thus identities can be used to help achieve personal and social recognition. At the same time, they can cause suffering to a subject through non-recognition or misrecognition which effects harms.

Social and queer theorist Judith Butler has taken up themes of identity and recognition in her scholarship. This chapter converses with selected works of Butler to show that practices of recognition are concerned with identity, but also with life and death itself. My central claim is that identity is best understood as a constellation, evoking the image of stars set in the night sky. Just like a constellation contains distinct stars that make a cohesive *interpreted* image and narrative, so too do our identities when they are viewed through the telescopes of another. Likewise, we can watch one star, one identity, within that constellation collapse and watch the constellation be shaped again, with new energy and matter. Constellations of identity are always slowly shifting. Because they are visible, they can be read by others as well as by the very subject who shapes the constellation. In fact, they must be visible in order for subjects to be socially intelligible.

We turn to identity primarily because there are both goods and ills to the way that identity works in the social, political, and theological realms. As a good, identity can bind individuals into groups of belonging, especially persons who have experienced similar oppressions based on identities. Having a social or political identity builds up the self-in-relation and fosters connection and resilience. Further, claiming identity in the public sphere enables individuals to collectively ask for recognition of social and political rights. However, social and political identity requires submission to systems of discourse, many of which borrow and bleed one from the other—political discourse, theological discourse, even medical discourse. Naming identities and injustices suffered (currently and historically) as a people is a vulnerable experience. In order to name an identity, the concept of a specific identity must be recognized by others who may not be part of that group of belonging. This concept of an identity, removed from specific people, is subject to manipulation, misinterpretation, and even physical violence. These harms are made possible by the fact that we are not solely our identities nor we do we completely control them. Rather, they are something distinct that we inhabit and learn how to be, or sometimes, how to manipulate by our own accord. We receive messages from the political, social, and theological world about the identities we inhabit—for example, messages of "yes, you are doing woman correctly," "no, you are not doing woman correctly," and "maybe, I'm not sure, I think you may (or may not) be doing woman correctly."

Doing or not doing woman correctly has direct implications for feminist pastoral theology. Gender is one lens of analysis which assists pastoral theologians to determine strategic interventions for just care. As an analytic category, gender functions to show us commonalities between those who suffer. What is additionally needed is an intersectional approach where gender is considered alongside other identities that place women at-risk, such as race or sexuality. Even then, analysis by identity becomes less than helpful when we mistake a theoretical analytical category for an experiential formation of the subject. For example, in my research with hospital chaplains I sought to describe female subjects of care and their suffering after fetal demise. I became critical of the chaplains' lack of an intersectional analysis of the women's identities and social locations, and how these factors impacted their experience of loss. I initially saw this as a problem of misrecognition that impacted the kind of care that women received. When I stepped back from my research, I was able to see that I asked about the category of identity as it if were something that the subjects did once and forever, instead of asking how they were done by, or submitted to, their identities. As a result, I missed a chance to analyze how they understood their subject formation and how they might have resisted their formation, particularly when experiencing suffering as result of who they were.

Even more, I faced a conundrum in trying to write about pastoral care through the lens of identity. Did I presume that all women displayed emotional outpourings of grief because I assumed that females were more natural or "in-touch" with their emotions? Did I presume that I could tell these women about the kind of care they needed because they seemed intelligible to me? Did I misrecognize them by fixing and solidifying identity even when assertions to the contrary were being made? By solidifying in my mind who counted as a woman in need of care, did I fail to recognize certain women, making them Other? In other words, I found myself in a Catch-22. I desired to analyze my findings through an intersectional approach using the categories of gender and race/ethnicity in order to give voice to the women whose suffering I thought was compounded by health injustices experienced as a result of ethnocentrism, racism, and classism. Yet, I was aware that my attempts to do this kind of analysis, even through a broad pastoral care lens, bordered on misrecognition and abstraction.

To be and become resilient people and communities in the face of suffering and injustice, we must understand how our identities can be both sites of subjectivation and sites of agency through the social process of recognition. In this chapter, I examine identity and recognition in three stages. First, I argue alongside Judith Butler that we learn to perform our identities through an iterative process, using gender as a locus for this discussion. Second, I contend that identity is a serious, lived game which is both a site for playfulness as well as potential harms that come from failing to perform identity correctly. Next, I argue that mourning and lament are central to the practice of recognition as they invite a reckoning with past and possible articulations of the self-in-relation. Last, I conclude the chapter with critiques of Butler and draw out implications for feminist pastoral theology.

## Performing Woman

Both critiqued and admired in the academy and in public life, Judith Butler is a third-wave feminist philosopher whose social theories ought not be ignored. Her writing examines broad and divergent topics including gender and sexuality, war and violence, and cultural politics. She draws from continental philosophy, literary theory, social and political theory, feminist theory, and queer theory, of which "she is regarded by many as *the* queer theorist par excellence" and a founder of the field.[2] She is a prolific writer, authoring, co-authoring, and editing over twenty books, and authoring numerous book chapters and countless articles. She is the subject of the film *Philosophical Encounters of the Third Kind* (2006) and featured in the film *The Examined Life* (2008).

Once a derogatory term for LGBT persons who challenged the heteronormative ideal, queer denotes a move away from binary categories such as gay/straight, woman/man, and connotes fluidity in sexual orientation and gender identity. Likewise, queer theory challenges the premise that sex and gender are essential categories that exist by genetic or divine decree. As anthropologist Tanya Erzen explains, "Instead, queer theory argues for the idea that identities are culturally and historically determined rather than fixed; sexual practices and desires change over time and do not consistently line up with masculine or feminine gender expectations."[3] In broader academic discourse queer theory deconstructs normalizing practices and institutions. It does not signal a sexual identity as such, but indicates an outlook that challenges hegemony, dominating discourses (including that of identity), and knowledge-power regimes.[4]

It is not unusual to hear theological conversations in which sex is described as fixed and anatomical, gender as flowing from sex, and sexuality arising from the blend of these two descriptions. There is an assumption that the presence of a penis makes someone a man, and that the lack makes someone a female. Drawing from natural law, the penis and thus the male's natural masculine desire is toward its opposite, a vagina and a female. Judith Butler reverses this way of thinking and argues that sexuality privileges heternormativity and that gender does not flow from anatomical sex. She is best known for her influential book *Gender Trouble: Feminism and the Subversion of Identity* (1990) in which she questioned whether "women," who it was assumed shared essential characteristics and interests, was the proper subject of feminism.[5] *Gender Trouble* not only pioneered new territory in feminist thought, but also

2. Salih, *Judith Butler*, 7.

3. Erzen, *Straight to Jesus*, 14.

4. Marshall, "Models of Understanding Differences," 37.

5. Armour and St. Ville, "Judith Butler in Theory," 1.

established itself as a foundational text in queer theory.[6] Working in the philosophical spirit of Michel Foucault and drawing from philosophers J. L. Austin and Jacques Derrida, Butler destabilizes the account of gender through her theory of performativity. In her account, gender is active. It is "a doing rather than a being."[7] Cause and effect are reversed in this theory. I do not "do" my gender. My gender does me. Gender, then, is not a performance that is freely chosen from myriad creative possibilities by a discrete subject. Instead, gender performance is a constraint that may also become a site for its undoing.

In *Gender Trouble* (1990), Butler argues that gender is an iterative performance, following from Simone de Beauvoir's statement that a woman is not born but made. The body is a permeable site where social and political systems of gender/sex significate themselves.[8] Whereas second-wave feminists argued against biological determinism by showing that sex does not determine gender roles, for example that an anatomical female may become a CEO of a Fortune 500 company, or that an anatomical male may become a house husband, Butler collapses sex/gender distinctions.[9] According to Butler, masculinity and femininity as gender "masquerade as natural" by pointing to the body's primary and secondary sex organs "as their signature and guarantee."[10] To say it another way, it is not our sex which determines our gender and sexuality. The presence of the penis does not illuminate masculinity, nor must it necessarily lead to heterosexual desire. Instead, "a social system of compulsory heterosexuality" shapes our desire, making us believe that gender and sex are two distinct and binary aspects of our subjectivity.[11]

The normative claims tend to go something like this: I do my gender correctly through my learned performance of "woman." To take on this role, I move a certain way with my body and wear certain kinds of clothes and shoes that reflect my gender. I react in certain kinds of ways to emotional overtones, such as caring for others at the expense of my own well-being. Because my vagina implies absence, I desire wholeness. I desire man (or the penis) which reaffirms my heterosexual desire. My religion

6. Ibid., viii.
7. Salih, *The Judith Butler Reader*, 90.
8. Butler, *Gender Trouble*, 189.
9. Armour and St. Ville, "Judith Butler in Theory," 2.
10. Ibid., 5.
11. Ibid.

confirms and regulates all of this with claims from natural law. My social and political life similarly confirms all this with legal precedents and state confirmed, heterosexual role models. Culture and media reassert and confirm this claim with advertising, images, and stories that sustain womanhood as the one thing of heterosexuality.

However, my perception of myself as vagina, woman, and heterosexual is a learned performance. I have been schooled by religion, politics, and social systems of family, community, and education. Thus, I am constituted as a woman when the social and political systems of gender/sex have acted upon me sufficiently enough to render me intelligible, or recognizable, as "woman." I repeat this performance day-in and day-out and thus I become intelligible as a woman because I live up to the social law of woman as heterosexual.

In learning my performance, it would seem that I become merely a reflection of cultural mores. However, this is not the case, per Butler. Because every performance of woman is an iteration of signifying practices, every performance is radically contingent. Woman is not naturally heterosexual or even anatomically female. Instead, woman is a set of normative practices that are reiterated over and over upon the subject, forming the subject into someone recognizable as a woman. This claim raises critical questions about who is recognized as a woman if woman is a socially constructed category in which selves-in-relation are shaped.

Must a "woman" always have to be anatomically female to be recognized as "woman"? Absolutely not, Butler answers. The practice of drag is an example of gender performativity that Butler uses. Drag queen performances—anatomical men performing woman (drag queens)—are locations where the lies of a "natural woman" are revealed. Drag shows the creative dissonance between anatomical sex, gender identity, and gender performance. Any woman can fail to do her gender correctly in all sorts of ways. A subject underperforms or overperforms woman and shows the contingency of gender. Using drag as an example, an anatomical man makes himself "woman" by clothing in make-up, pantyhose, brassieres, and high heels. She may "fool" the man on the street. Were that man on the street to recognize the drag queen as a male/man "masquerading" as a woman, we assume that he would judge her performance a failure. However, instead of judging her performance as a failure to perform "woman" correctly, we are urged by Butler to consider how no one ever measures up to the heterosexual (and white, able-bodied, and upper-middle class) ideologies that constitute woman. Every body is a gender outlaw.

There is excitement, or "giddiness"[12] in the words of Butler, when we realize that all our bodily performances are drag. Whether we have the "correct" body parts, skin color, gait, or size, not one of us follows the recipe of gender to the letter of the law. In fact, the letter of the gender law is fiction. Butler uses the phrase "regulatory fiction" to describe what is often held as a true gender identity but which she argues is made through social performance. And yet, this fiction regulates our lives with consequences as to the possibilities of life we can imagine, and those we cannot.[13] Regulatory fiction, when lived out, may cause harm, maiming, and even death of the other who does not live up to the fictive ideal.

## Identity is Serious

Any body which does not perform woman (or man) correctly is subject to othering, abjection, or expulsion. Butch women are too manly. Black women are not white enough. Lesbians are not heterosexual. Their performances of woman do not measure up. According to Butler, the ideology of woman cannot tolerate deviations and thus expels any body which exposes the ideology of the idealized woman. The case of Nina Davaluri, a former Miss America, shows us what happens when the ideology of woman is exposed as regulatory fiction.

Nina Davuluri was named Miss America in September 2013. An Indian American and former Miss New York, Davuluri was the subject of tweets declaring her a terrorist and Arab—a misreading of her brown body as a terrorist, Muslim body from the Arabian Peninsula. Other tweets made crude jokes about her as "Miss 7–11"—a classist and religiously ignorant reading of her ethnic heritage. Though now illegal, the caste system of Hinduism, the indigenous religion of the Indian subcontinent, directs the occupations of members within a caste. Occupation as a shopkeeper is a long part of the Vaishya or merchant caste. While the tweets were quickly called racist, they expose the operative norms of sex/gender within a constellation of identities. The idealized woman—who other than "Miss America"?—ought to be non-ethnic (read white) and thoroughly American (read middle-class and Christian). Davuluri responded by emphasizing her Miss American platform to promote diversity through education.

12. Butler, *Gender Trouble*, 187.
13. Ibid., 192.

The case of Davuluri exposes how the ideal of woman has serious consequences for all selves-in-relation. If everybody that has a body never quite measures up, then the ideal is not only unattainable, but denigrating to all bodies. Not measuring up could go a number of ways. If we are done by our identities, as Butler argues, our failures to recognize performances of woman as something other than the regulatory ideal mark a lack of imaginative capacity. Acknowledging our necessary failures as finite and contingent human beings may lead to opportunities for us to see how no one measures up, and thus increase our capacity for empathic relationships and recognition of others. Acknowledging our failures may cause us to resist the hegemony of gender ideals which limit our imaginative capacities. Being a subject who does not measure up but believes in her inherent self-worth and dignity may increase resiliency. However, neither recognition nor resiliency is guaranteed, particularly when our performances are deemed deviant.

Performances are not costumes or clothes. Gender/sex identities cannot be taken on and off, like sweaters or shoes or pantyhose. They are constructed but also given. So, while I may choose to enact a gender performance of a certain type, there are limits to my intelligibility. Like the drag queen's Adam's apple, my body may give me away in all sorts of ways I had never imagined possible. As such, performativity is a delimiting concept rather than one which allows for the making and unmaking of all gender, as if all gender and sex options were available in the fictional closet. It is actually the constraint of performing my gender that makes it possible to perform. Like the chicken and the egg, I perform woman because there is an ideal, or regulatory fiction of woman that has structured my self-understanding. And yet, there are possibilities for resistance through deviation.[14]

Performative possibilities are deviations—both intentional and unintentional. Deviation of a correct gender or sex performance makes possible alternatives for doing and undoing gender/sex. However, deviation from reiterated norms comes at a price. A subject may become unintelligible and unrecognized at multiple levels of scale, or worse, may experience violence, injustice, and oppression as a consequence of lack of recognition. For example, as I dress, walk, and talk, I do not consciously reflect on whether I am doing "woman" correctly. I believe that the way I act is natural, given, unchallengeable. Yet, it is because of the ways that I

14. Butler, *Bodies That Matter*, 94.

am interpreted—in my case, specifically as white and heterosexual—that enable my performance to be recognized and conferred with a yes of social recognition. What of bodies whose performance is met with a no or a maybe? When met with a no, Davuluri resisted the words aimed at her by using her own words to advocate for diversity education. When body meets body and a no is given, there are times when neither resilience nor resistance is possible. Hate crimes, like the brutal beating and death of transgendered women in Brazil, make this case.

While we hope that performances enable resilience, resilience does not necessarily follow. To say it another way, the identities we inhabit are always already sites of subjectivation as well as agency. Subjectivation and agency are not only concepts but lived responses to oppressive, unjust forces. We experience both oppression and agency through our identities. This is especially true when our multiple and overlapping identities are read through each other, set in a constellation of power that maps itself on our bodies to which all discursive systems respond through recognition, misrecognition, or no recognition. Subjects who occupy multiple planes of identity are confronted by the ideological apparati that may confer recognition if the subject performs correctly enough, deny recognition, or enable misrecognition in the form of passing. Categories of identity cannot be neatly unpacked and deideologized because the subjects who inhabit and are inhabited by identities do not live their lives as separate categories of existence.

Butler's analysis of the character Claire from the short story *Passing* by Nella Larsen, illuminates these serious questions. By serious I mean to imply, along with the anthropologist Sherry B. Ortner, that no matter what clothes we put on, or how we learn to act, our lives are always on the line. Yet, there can be excitement—a rush—that we feel when we game the system.[15] We may feel giddy when we consciously come to

15. Ortner, *Making Gender*, 12. Ortner offers serious game as a theory of practice. She writes, "The idea of the 'game' is meant to capture simultaneously the following dimensions: that social life is culturally organized and constructed, in terms of defining categories of actors, rules and goals of the games, and so forth; that social life is precisely social, consisting of webs of relationship and interaction between multiple, shifting interrelated subject positions, none of which can be extracted as autonomous 'agents'; and yet at the same time there is 'agency', that is, actors play with skill, intention, wit, knowledge, intelligence. The idea that the game is 'serious' is meant to add into the equation the idea that power and inequality pervade the games of life in multiple ways, and that, while there is playfulness and pleasure in the process, the stakes of these games are often very high. It follows in turn that the games of life must be played with intensity and sometimes deadly earnestness."

understand that breaking the rules may lead to alternative visions of how to live. Still, we may not always acknowledge more serious consequences which lead to psychic and physical violence and exploitation. Moreover, discursive systems inform us of that yes, that no, that maybe, and effect how we evaluate ourselves even as we attempt to embody alternative visions. Discursive systems also inform how we are interpreted by other people that we encounter in the coffee shop, at church, at the night club, at our places of employment, and as we navigate our social world. When I dress in certain ways or act in certain ways that challenge social codes that, though constructed have become sedimented, I may be snubbed, punished, dominated, or even killed. On the other hand, it could be that my performance—again, which never measures up—is a place of resistance, of resilience, of creative possibilities in the everyday practice of life.

In the essay "Passing, Queering: Nella Larsen's Psychoanalytic Challenge," Butler argues that identities are not to be read as distinct listings to be set off by commas—gender, sexuality, race, class—but as signifiers upon signifiers of power, agency, and recognition that are visible and hidden at the same time. Analyzing power at the point of convergence yields information about the ways that identities work together to mask what the ideological law would hold as a less than good-enough performance of the ideal. That is, we must learn to read identity as a constellation—distinct stars set in the night sky which give shape to an apparent set form, but which are actually in motion, may not even be visible, and thus are not set in a certain everlasting form. Butler shows us how to do this when she rereads Nella Larsen's short story *Passing*.

Larsen's short story *Passing* raises questions about the visible and the hidden. "The question of what can and cannot be spoken, what can and cannot be publicly exposed, is raised throughout the text, and it is linked with the larger question of the dangers of public exposure of both color and desire," Butler writes.[16] We are introduced to several characters: Clare, Bellew, and Irene. Clare is the main character who passes as both white and straight, and as such her passing in both senses "signifies a certain freedom, a class mobility afforded by whiteness."[17] Bellew is Clare's racist, white husband. Irene is Clare's friend who also passes as white and straight. The climax of the story occurs when Bellew spots Clare and Irene together in an all black Harlem salon.

16. Butler, *Bodies That Matter*, 169.
17. Ibid., 170.

Butler argues that Clare's passing in white circles must be considered in light of her straightness and class assumptions. "Clare passes not only because she is light-skinned, but because she refuses to introduce her blackness into conversation, and so withholds the conversational marker which would counter the hegemonic presumption that she is white."[18] In her white social circles, her blackness is not called to account because her body cannot be read. As Butler notes, "What can be seen, what qualifies as a visible marking, is a matter of being able to read a marked body in relation to unmarked bodies, where unmarked bodies constitute the currency of normative whiteness."[19] To say it another way, because Clare acts white and appears white, there is no question of her whiteness. Her body is perceived as an unmarked body because she carries herself as white and middle class. She passes and she is misrecognized. Her misrecognition benefits her social status.

Her misrecognition is also perpetuated by the person whom we might assume would see her most clearly, her husband Bellew. Perceived as white, she receives recognition from her overtly racist husband, who claims that he would never associate with blacks. Paradoxically, his ability to recognize her as white is fueled by his vehement racism. In his psyche he experiences blackness as bad and whiteness as good, a dangerous psychic split that enables him to embody his whiteness as a pure identity. Butler explains, Bellew "cannot be white without blacks and without the constant disavowal of his relation to them. It is only through that disavowal that his whiteness is perpetually—but anxiously—reconstituted."[20]

Passing does not remove the inhabited identities that constitute the subject, but instead enlists intersubjective misinterpretation and misrecognition to uphold the normative ideal. For example, Butler implies that Clare's body is not fully under her own control, even in its passing. Though her blackness becomes visible to her racist husband Bellew when he sees her in the company of other black-skinned persons in a Harlem salon, there are intimations of her blackness from Bellew before this time. He calls her "Nig" as a pet name; he says that she is becoming more dark-skinned day by day.[21]

18. Ibid., 171.
19. Ibid., 170.
20. Ibid., 171.
21. Ibid.

Yet Bellew does not actively name her blackness. To do so would mean that the distinct categories of black as bad and white as good that he desires are not possible in the body of the one he loves without exposing his investment in that dichotomy. When Bellew does not consciously allow himself to see Clare's blackness, he can unconsciously desire her as his fetish object. He desires her blackness even when he says he does not want it. His denied desire eroticizes Clare and makes her more and more an object, something to be conquered and dominated. Her subjugation as an exotic object is made possible by his perceptions of her racial ambivalence. This serious game of personal and social recognition has consequences. As Bellow sees Clare in an all black Harlem salon, he must confront his own racism. He cannot see in her what he cannot consider for himself.[22]

As the veneer of Clare's whiteness disintegrates, so too does her assumed heterosexuality. Sitting next to her, on the precipice of the window in the Harlem salon, is Irene. Irene is another light-skinned black who passes, but who is ambiguous about her passing. With equal ambiguity, Irene desires Clare and a relational way of being outside the scope of heteronormativity. Yet she also denies her desire at the very same time. Butler writes, "Clare embodies a certain kind of sexual daring that Irene defends herself against . . . and Irene finds herself drawn by Clare, wanting to be her, but also wanting her."[23] After Bellew sees her, Clare falls out the salon window to her death. The reader is left to wonder if Irene played a role in Clare's death. In her denial of what she cannot have, what she may never been able to dream of having, does Irene push Clare so far away that she falls to her death?

In reading *Passing* with Butler we learn that intersubjective recognition is not guaranteed, even by those who say they love us and with whom we have committed ourselves as partners. When recognition is not positively conferred, our subjectivity borders on misrecognition in its search to overcome non-recognition. Further, our ability to be recognized by another subject is tied to our ability to be recognized by social institutions. Social institutions, like marriage, may be enlisted as both a site of subjectivation as well as a site of resistance as bodies and identities are misrecognized or not recognized at all. Our being recognized by another correlates to their understanding of our intersectional performance

22. Ibid., 173.
23. Ibid., 169.

of gender/sex, race, and class. And yet, our recognition is also partly based on that other's ability to reckon with their own disavowal. Bellew could not recognize his love, Clare, because he could not reckon with his own racism. As we will see, we must enlist the work of mourning in order to reckon with those lived identities which might otherwise lead to disavowal of another.

## Being Done and Undone

Suffering comes to all, loss is inevitable, and grief beckons. Some choose to relish in the grief and to feel it fully, exploring the contours and dimensions of an emotion that always feels, while in its midst, without end. And this is an uncomfortable feeling—the waves of grief that arise without our calling to them. We can choose, we seem to think, to turn the waves back and stop the sea of loss. Yet, a lack of emotional response to loss is a loss in itself.

In *Giving An Account of Oneself*, Butler argues that recognition is an ethical project based on failure and opacity.[24] The descriptions we give of ourselves are contingent. They are predicated upon norms into which we have been born. Thus, while we might insist on saying that we have "chosen" to become something, this choosing is illusory. At the same time, deviations in our performance make room for new possibilities. Every time that we say we have chosen an identity, we reveal the limitations of the making of that identity even as our performances fail and show the making of norms. Even more, certain ways that we give accounts of ourselves, such as the way Clare tells about herself, both by what she says and cannot say, both by what she performs and what she cannot perform, show how identities are maps of power, as well as how they might be recharted. In doing so, we reveal to others as well as to ourselves the identities which we inhabit and which inhabit us. We reveal who we understand ourselves to be and who we hope to become.

However, to give a full account of ourselves is impossible. We do not fully know ourselves in the present moment. Nor do we fully know the selves of our becoming in the future. Nor do we know if the language, and social and political structures available to us will render us unintelligible to others, or maybe even to ourselves. Yet, we are called to account for

---

24. Butler, *Giving An Account of Oneself*, 21.

ourselves.[25] Our accounting of ourselves is imperfect. We recognize that our own imperfect or unknown self-knowledge may result in a failure to be understood when we try to give an account of ourselves. When we try to give accounts of others, we are even more stymied. For Butler, this conclusion leads to ethics in intellectual inquiry as well as practice.

Butler argues that given the sustained failure to know the selves that we are becoming and the selves that others are becoming, we must suspend judgment of self and of others. Because there are pieces of one's self that have become othered through the process of splitting, the suspension of self-judgment calls into being a destabilized and reflexive self. She is a subject who pauses in the midst of her assertions and petitions for recognition because she acknowledges the limitations of fully knowing herself. If she cannot fully give an account of herself, then giving a full account of another is equally difficult. Thus, an ethical practice of recognition "obligates us to suspend judgment in order to apprehend the other."[26]

Suspending judgment is a relational act, as is judging, and both enact an ethic which is visible in rhetoric. For example, judging is enacted by the mode of address. The words spoken tell us something about the nature of the relationship between selves and the relationship one has with one's self. Butler gives us the example of condemnation to show us how a mode of address may deny recognition and the consequences to the subject formation of the one who condemns. As forms of rhetorical address, condemnation, denunciation, and excoriation "posit an ontological difference between judge and judged."[27] Butler explains, "Condemnation becomes the way in which we establish the other as nonrecognizable or jettison some aspect of ourselves that we lodge in the other, whom we then condemn."[28] What would we learn about the interior life of the individuals who called Davuluri a terrorist or Miss 7–11, if we heard their own accounts of self? Like domination, condemnation limits self-knowledge by creating greater disparity between the disavowed and the judger. If the judger can see no commonality between herself and another, then her own self-knowledge becomes even more opaque.

Like domination, condemnation enacts violence against another subject. It purges and externalizes one's own opacity, so that it is not part of one's own self but instead removed. For example, Bellew projects his

25. Ibid.
26. Ibid., 44.
27. Ibid, 46.
28. Ibid.

vehement racism outward in his inability to understand his own desires. He judges and condemns the personification of blackness that he desires but that he will not acknowledge in himself. Not only does he split blackness-whiteness into all good-all bad, he also splits himself, condemning the blackness in which he has made his home in marriage. Just as he cannot see that he is limited, he also cannot see that other human beings may be just as limited. His judgment is misrecognition. It stems from a failure to recognize the limitations in our knowing of ourselves as well as others who are in proximity to us.

Like other limitations and failures, lack of self-knowledge calls for grief work, mourning, and lamentation. However, by its very nature, the ability to mourn our lack of self-knowledge is difficult. We cannot mourn that which we cannot acknowledge. Yet acknowledging what you do not know about yourself is challenging, but not impossible. In order to mourn what we are not when a future possibility forecloses—the straight man who must acknowledge that he will never ever be gay—requires self-reflexive knowledge and terrible self-insight. Terrible self-insight comes by practicing self-extended futuring as I imagine my life performance as someone that I would like to disavow. While empathy would have us stand in another person's shoes, however imperfect our understanding, self-extended futuring demands imaginative risk and a willingness to be in discomfort. What happens when I ask, what if I were to live my life as a gay woman? When I ask myself this question, indeed when any of us ask this kind of self-extended futuring question, our answer requires us to come out to ourselves. There is an internal good to our discomfort. We cannot grieve that which we do not wish to acknowledge as a possibility in ourselves. Otherwise, we may cast internal otherness outward in judgment. We misrecognize another person when we fail to imagine how personal and social identities shape another's movement through the world.

We may deny recognition to other subjects when our internalized otherness is not cast-out, but instead goes unrecognized and unacknowledged. Instead of misrecognition, it is non-recognition. Non-recognition, like misrecognition, is an injustice to one's self and to another. Non-recognition results in an inability to grieve one's life or another's life. It is a state of deep opacity in which one no longer stretches out her hands to feel for another, but surrenders to the inky darkness in which no emotions of grief or injustice can reinstate an ethical relationship.

In her 2004 book *Precarious Life*, Butler asks, "What makes for a grievable life?"[29] We might rephrase and ask, why are some lives not mourned? Following from an ethic of rhetoric, she indicates that subjects become ungrievable by prohibitive speech acts. For example, in 2002 a Palestinian citizen of the United States submitted obituaries of two families killed by Israeli troops. The *San Francisco Chronicle* refused to run the obituaries without proof of death. In lieu of obituaries, they stated that memoriams could be submitted to the paper. After revision, the memoriams were rejected as well "with the explanation that the newspaper did not wish to offend anyone."[30]

The refusal to acknowledge the deaths publicly in speech is the violence of non-recognition enacted on those who were killed. It is not their deaths that are offensive to others, but their lives, which will not be written as "lost." Instead, there is omission, nothing, as if there were no bodies. Butler observes that the "refusal of discourse"[31] dehumanizes them as subjects. They are made victims twice-over, first in their deaths and again in the public's inability to be confronted by their deaths. Their lives are erased in a physical and literal sense. We cannot publicly grieve. This is violence by omission and does harm to both human life and human imagination.

Without public grief, we become closed, static, and fixed. A refusal or inability to grieve forecloses moments of vulnerability when one may be truly challenged, rearranged, or transformed. Butler writes, "One mourns when once accepts that by the loss one undergoes one will be changed, possibly for ever. Perhaps mourning has to do with agreeing to undergo a transformation (perhaps one should say submitting to a transformation) the full result of which one cannot know in advance."[32] Undergoing grief, mourning the loss of another's life, and mourning what never was in our lives reveals the ties that "constitute what we are . . . that compose us."[33] Grief interrupts the carefully constructed narrative that we give of ourselves-in-relationship. Butler explains, "What grief displays . . . is the thrall in which our relations with others hold us, in ways that we cannot always recount or explain, in ways that often interrupt the

29. Butler, *Precarious Life*, 20.

30. Ibid., 35.

31. Ibid.

32. Ibid., 21.

33. Ibid., 22.

self-conscious account of ourselves we might try to provide, in ways that challenge the very notion of ourselves as autonomous and in control."[34] The I that I was before loss is different from the I that I am now. I recognize that I am different somehow through the loss, through the foreclosure, of the other's life. I am also made different in the foreclosure of how our lives together might have been, reflecting the relationship with others that constitute us as subjects.

Our ability to mourn the lives of others is directly tied to our ability to mourn our own lives. It is our ability to mourn and to grieve that elicits the conditions for recognition. For recognition is not only about the present, but also about the future which holds both possibility and foreclosure. Butler writes, "To ask for recognition, or to offer it, is precisely not to ask for recognition for what one already is. It is to solicit a becoming, to instigate a transformation, to petition the future always in relation to the Other."[35] To become a recognized subject requires that one mourn and grieve in order to allow space for intrapsychic self-in-relation transformation. It is an assertion of loss.

We assert our losses because they reflect the poverty of our relationships. When we mourn the unjust death of a vulnerable person who experiences multiple jeopardies of interlocking oppressions and structural violence, we signal that we are unwilling immediate participants who actively seek transformation. We petition the future (and other subjects of the future) to recognize subjects who are misrecognized or not recognized at all. I petition future selves-in-relation, including myself, because I am formed, informed, deformed, and reformed by my ethical relationships with others. My self is a self-in-relation, and my being is constituted by what multiple other subjects, not just myself, can imagine as possibilities for future living.

Recognizing other subjects in feminist pastoral theology requires that we name the binds in which we find ourselves in our personal and social spheres. In primary relationships with caregivers, deformation to the subject occurs in relationship to physical and psychosocial needs. The infant becomes an I through recognition of self-worth by another. Yet we know that not all infants have a primary caretaker whose face reflects joy and delight upon meeting face to face with the human infant. Instead, many experience emotional paucity or emotional abuse, often alongside

34. Ibid., 23.
35. Ibid., 44.

additional co-factors of economic vulnerability, political instability, and social misrecognition or non-recognition, as well as compounding experiences of oppression and marginalization.[36] At the socio-political level, we also find ourselves in binds when we do not know whom to mourn because we do not know of their existence. Butler urges us to identify the "cultural barriers against which we struggle when we try to find out about the losses that we are asked not to mourn."[37] We must mourn, not only for our own becoming, but for the becoming of other selves-in-relation.

## Critiques and Implications for Feminist Pastoral Theology

Judith Butler's theoretical work is crucial to developing theories of subjectivity in feminist pastoral theology as she provides rich engagement on concepts of identity performance, how identities are articulated through each other, interpersonal and social recognition, and mourning. However, she is not without her critics who argue that she normalizes familial and social oppression as necessary conditions for agency.

After *Gender Trouble* was published, philosopher Martha Nussbaum penned a response to Butler's claims. In "The Professor of Parody," Nussbaum parallels Butler's dense writing style with the style used by ancient sophist rhetoricians. She argues that Butler's writing obscures the line of argument and "bullies" the reader into accepting the propositions and their conclusions.[38] In addition to writing in a difficult to understand style, Nussbaum argues that Butler's theorizing hurts women by removing any normative turn toward a feminist ethic rooted in correcting social injustices or advancing human dignity. What Butler offers is "quietism and retreat" from the most pressing problems that face women. [39]

---

36. Ibid., 45. Butler writes, "This bind of radically inadequate care consists of this, namely, that attachment is crucial to survival and that, when attachment takes place, it does so in relation to persons and institutional conditions that may well be violent, impoverishing, and inadequate." While the child psychologist D. W. Winnicott explains that maternal failure ought to be expected and is necessary for child development in his concept of the good-enough mother, Butler is making a distinction between optimal failure necessary for self-growth and the reality of inadequate care which would far exceed optimal failure.

37. Ibid., 46.

38. Nussbaum, "The Professor of Parody," para 13.

39. Ibid.., para 7.

While Nussbaum's attack was particularly vitriolic, it captured a sentiment shared by feminists who linked theorizing with social action. How does the claim that "woman" or "lesbian" as a series of citational performances help those who suffer in material ways and who do not yet possess sufficient power to make social and political changes that translate into changes in their everyday live? Does not this claim strip women of their agency to create significant social and political strides? Are parody and difficult prose real tools for social change?

Butler engages these critiques in her subsequent writing projects. In her 1999 preface to *Gender Trouble*, Butler informed the reader that her theories were informed by social experience and social concern. "Despite the dislocation of the subject that the text performs, there is a person here: I went to many meetings, bars, and marches, and saw many kinds of genders, understood myself to be at the crossroads of some of them, and encountered sexuality at several of its cultural edges," she writes.[40] Likewise, after the publication of *Gender Trouble*, she heard from many persons outside of the academy who, though conceding it a difficult read, "also felt that something was at stake in that theoretical work that made the reading worthwhile."[41] In an interview, Butler explains that reading her theoretical work is difficult because it destabilizes everyday usage of language.[42] In this way, language may become a tool for social action by opening up linguistic possibilities of refutation, leading us to imagine a different world and to take pragmatic political action that calls the world into being.[43] However, a fundamental question remains. If language is destabilized to make odd what was once normal, is the remaining desta-bilized and complex language available to those who are subjectivated at the psychological and material level?

Likewise, Butler is prescient of feminist political anxiety. If the feminist subject cannot be said to exist as such, how can any political praxis which seeks to rectify perceived gendered injustice persist? Butler responds to this anxiety by reiterating that subject construction does not remove agency. "Construction is not opposed to agency; it is the neces-sary scene of agency, the very terms in which agency is articulated and

40.  Butler, *Gender Trouble*, xvi.

41.  Breen et al, "There is a Person Here," 23.

42.  Ibid.

43.  Brookey and Miller, "Changing Signs," 139–53.

becomes culturally intelligible."[44] Gender performances that stretch the limits of intelligibility are possible critical interventions. Rather than globalize the subject through use of imperial strategies, strategies which "feminism ought to criticize,"[45] the political subject who is aware of the construction of gender is an agent who can utilize the tools of gender inscribed through the body to contest the matrix of an idealized gendered woman: heterosexual, anatomically female, and white. These are subversive acts of an agent whose subjectivity is unstable from the first. Through repetitive performances, the subject both does and undoes gender and herself at the same time.[46] Performances are variations on the idealized subject and thus can potentially make visible the cultural apparatus that inscribes the rules of a good or bad gender performance and enables subjects to do their performance another way.

Academics, in addition to Nussbaum, have wondered how to put Butler's theory to work in politics. They argue that bodily-linguistic performances and ongoing performance failures ought to be understood as resistance, and by resistance, hope for personal and political change that works by coalition rather than as assumed identity by gender, race, ability, etc. However, this conclusion does not necessarily follow from Butler's writing in *Gender Trouble*, a point that Nussbaum makes in her scathing critique. Nussbaum writes, "There is a void, then, at the heart of Butler's notion of politics. This void can look liberating, because the reader fills it implicitly with a normative theory of human equality or dignity. But let there be no mistake: for Butler, as for Foucault, subversion is subversion, and it can in principle go in any direction."[47]

Nussbaum, like many critics of deconstruction, is anxious about the void and its results for the subject. Three questions arise that are worth exploring with theological thinkers who draw on Butler. First, is this void an empty space for Butler that can be filled within anything? Second, is there some kind of ethical vision that this space holds open? Third, what does the void of gender/sex and additional analytic categories of identity mean for subjects who experience injustice? To the first and second questions, Butler's later writing articulates an ethos that critiques exclusion. Empty space exists, but it exists for the future possibilities that we cannot

44. Butler, *Gender Trouble*, 201.

45. Ibid.

46. Ibid., 195.

47. Nussbaum, "The Professor of Parody," para. 37.

yet imagine but which we petition by attending to the present's dimensions of othering. In doing so, we petition future becomings oriented toward justice. She writes in *Bodies That Matter*, "The task is to refigure this necessary 'outside' as a future horizon, one in which the violence of exclusion is perpetually in the process of being overcome."[48] The void is not empty, but full of contingency and possibility. It can never rule out the possibility of failure or exclusion even while moving toward more liberative ways of being.

This question of the void is serious, particularly in a pastoral theological context, and I find British theological ethicist Susan F. Parsons helpful in attending to it. In "The Boundaries of Desire," Parsons writes that Butler's gender theorizing is "a move beyond ethics, of after ethics, into what is a spirituality of living towards an open horizon."[49] She explains that if we accept the proposition that even the best attempts at ethical reasoning are shaped by and reinforce the hegemonic imagination and law which excludes, there is a need to think through matters differently. Different thinking leads to different living—temporal living, transcendent living, living with Nothing according to Parsons. At the edges of transcendent living is the acceptance of contingency, "an awareness that the orders in which we find ourselves might not be as they are."[50] Parson concludes that transcendant living touches relationships with friends where we hold open space for becoming, and living in such a way is closely tied to the "deep wisdom of Christian prayer."[51]

In constructing subjectivity in feminist pastoral theology, the dissolution of an ontological feminist subject asks us to assess the validity of Butler's theories in the face of oppression and injustice. Womanist theologian Karen Baker-Fletcher offers serious critique: "While White feminists are busy deconstructing self, Black women are still claiming the selves that a racist, sexist, classist society relentlessly essays to render invisible."[52] However, pastoral theologian Pamela Cooper-White offers a positive take on the dissolution of the essential woman. She writes, "It is precisely because these categories are finally constructs, and not immutable facts of nature, that gaps and inconsistencies within them may

48. Butler, *Bodies That Matter*, 53.

49. Parsons, "The Boundaries of Desire," 103.

50. Ibid., 104.

51. Ibid.

52. Baker-Fletcher, "The Erotic in Contemporary Black Women's Writings," 199.

provide spaces from which both women and racialized, subaltern, and queered subjects can speak."[53] The voices from the gaps cast doubt on the working of the idealized norm making machine. As such, "subjugated voices can erode and 'jam the machinery' of dominance much the way fluids can erode seemingly solid rock."[54] The implication of a stance like Cooper-White's requires that we hold loosely universal moral imperatives and instead contextualize them through the intersections of the life of the subject, intersections which are constituted in and through their performance and petitioning of the yet-unknown. This stands in contrast to ethical and pastoral projects that begin in the assumptions of moral imperatives for sexual or gendered conduct.[55]

For philosopher Kelly Oliver, Butler's theory of subjectivity is problematic because it assumes a hostility between persons as the condition for recognition. Hostility begets an alienation in which transformation of power structures is made impossible.[56] Oliver writes, "By insisting that the structure of subjectivity is one of subjection and subordination, Butler builds oppression and abuse into the foundation of subjectivity."[57] Oliver's critique hinges upon a different reading of primary attachments in the family of origin. Per Oliver, Butler normalizes the trauma caused by subordination to a child's primary attachments. Oliver writes, "Trauma is the essential feature of these formative familial relations that set up the possibility of subjectivity. It is the trauma of original subordination that is repeated in all performances of subjectivity."[58] The problem for Oliver is that subordination and dependency are not synonymous; dependency need not result in subordination. Oliver explains,

> Why does dependency have to be figured as violent, alienating,
> subjugating, and dominating? Only if we start with the ideal of
> the self-possessed autonomous subject is dependence threaten-
> ing. If, however, we give up that ideal and operate in the world

53. Cooper-White, "Com\plicated Woman," 149.

54. Ibid.

55. Rudy, *Sex and the Church*, 123–25. Queer theory is perceived from some theological and institutional church circles as promoting a permissive, anything goes sexuality based completely on acts of pleasure of the individual. I believe that they misinterpret queer theory more generally as a theory without ethics rather than pointing to the ways that exclusion and binary codes function.

56. Oliver, *Witnessing*, 76.

57. Ibid., 62.

58. Ibid, 65. See Butler, *The Psychic Life of Power*, 7–9.

with a truly interrelational conception of subjectivity, a subjectivity without subjects, then dependence is seen as the force of life, as the very possibility of change, rather than as the paradoxical life bought at the expense of violence and death (Oliver 1998). Subjectivity need not be the Faustian bargain struck by Butler.[59]

In her reading of Butler, Oliver sees that a need for primary caretakers must result in subordination and that subordination by primary caretakers is necessary for subjectivity. Arguing against this reading, Oliver asks us to envision subject formation made possible by witnessing, a process which can be destroyed or damaged through subordination and trauma.[60] However, as Butler has noted in recent work, the bind of radically inadequate care must be considered in light of subject formation.

How does Butler's theory of subjectivity, especially her account of recognition, further refine feminist pastoral theological anthropology, and where might feminist pastoral theological anthropology offer other considerations? Judith Butler assures us that there is a person behind her theorizing, but is her notion of the person adequate? Butler's critics have implied that it is not. Nussbaum reminds us that descriptions of persons ought to enable their capacity to live better, free from poverty and violence. Oliver reminds us that childhood trauma ought not be the cause for our becoming subjects. However, Parsons sees the potential for transcendent living in Butler's work. Cooper-White describes subaltern, minority, and oppressed subjects of a Butlerian stripe whose voices confront dominators.

Through dialogue with Butler I hope I have conveyed what is at stake in questions of identity: not just life and death, although this is central, but also the question of what kind of lives are even recognizable as lives. We must mourn all lives if we are to reckon with the depths of social suffering, and our complicity and participation in the regulatory fiction that values some lives while denigrating others. Mourning all lives, all deficits, all failures requires that we mourn these things within ourselves. Terrible self-insight prompted by imaginative risk and self-extended futuring enables mourning and lament for identities that we might never consider for ourselves. These are identities which we stigmatize or condemn through speech—"retard," "fag," "Miss 7–11," "Nig"—because they

59. Ibid., 68.
60. Ibid., 7.

fail to live up to the hegemonic ideal of the white, straight, educated, Christian male, who is, himself, an illusion. A forced reiteration of norms constrains self-imagination and forecloses self-transformation, as well as communal imagination and transformation. Further, the forced reiteration of norms is enlisted to enable misrecognition or non-recognition of another. The regulatory fiction is then perceived as God-given truth requiring our assent. The latter is a dangerous proposition that not only denies multiplicity in forms of human flourishing, but limits our possibility to ascertain the very nature of God's self. The opaqueness of our self-in-relation extends to other human beings as well as God. As a result, we give a yes, a no, or a maybe to other human beings, to ourselves, and to God based on identities which do us even as we try to do them.

In the next chapter, I continue to investigate theories of recognition in reflecting on subject formation. I both appreciate and critique the work of liberation theologian Marcella Althaus-Reid who argues that liberation theology for a new generation requires analysis of sex/gender systems in order to adequately inform liberative theological discourse.

# 5

## *Theological Recognition*

In the preceding chapters, I have argued that recognition is a critical task for both human development and for the advancement of social justice. In dialogue with Benjamin and Butler, I have shown that subjects can be recognized, misrecognized, or not recognized at all. Impediments to human growth and the advancement of a more just world occur when subjects are misrecognized or not recognized at all. It is also critical to remember that misrecognition and non-recognition are part of the recognition spectrum. Thus, misrecognition or non-recognition, especially between subjects, can fill the hole where optimal recognition should be.

Just as subjects suffer from intersubjective and social misrecognition and non-recognition, so too can they suffer from theological misrecognition or non-recognition. Black theology, liberation theology, womanist theology, mujerista theology, lgbt inclusive theology, and queer theology bear testimony to the corrections needed within theology. Pastoral theology, too, has followed this trajectory, and especially feminist pastoral theology, where over the past 30 years the field has expanded from a white, mainline Protestant woman's perspective to something less unified and much more diverse, with the inclusion of voices speaking from a Roman Catholic, Evangelical, Korean, American Indian, African, Black, Puerto Rican, LGBTQ perspective, and varied socio-economic classes. I take this movement as a boon to theological discourse. Still, we know that there continue to be voices that do not speak or are not heard. In other words, they are misrecognized or not recognized at all. Again, a short case helps to contextualize how this critique plays out in the course of theologizing about human experience.

John was a doctoral student in chemical engineering when I first met him. He was schooled by Jesuits through high school and devoutly Roman Catholic, Chinese-Canadian, and male in gender presentation. Presently, I call him Sarah and she prefers to be known as a woman, though she still is closeted in many respects. When we talk, she asks me questions that demand theological reflection on the questions of who is recognized, misrecognized, and not recognized in theology and what this vital process of recognition means to the lives of all God's people. One question in particular stands out: "Does God allow my pining to be all woman?"[1] Her intensely personal question reveals the shape of het-eronormative theological practice and discourse. Can Sarah show up to liturgy as herself, not merely seen as a man masquerading as a woman, as confused, as in need of God's intervention in her life to make her gender expression and sexual desires "normal"? Will she be chastised directly or obliquely by those who minister? Sarah asserts herself and awaits recognition.

In this chapter, I argue that certain subjectivities, especially persons whose sexual or gender desire are outside the heteronormative spectrum of acceptability, may be subject to misrecognition and no recognition at all within theological discourse. I am aided in this assertion by the significant, thought-provoking work of Marcella Althaus-Reid, who before her death in 2009 developed a liberation theology attentive to sexual subjects and a queer God. As a theologian trained in liberation theology in South America, her scholarship broke new ground by exploring how liberative social and theological economies maintain the status quo and reproduce patriarchal norms. In this chapter, I first situate Althaus-Reid's contribution to theology in light of liberation theology, and argue that her scholarship contributes toward a theology of recognition. Second, with Althaus-Reid I describe how normative images of God and the Divine life (read: white, upper middle class, educated, straight, male) constrain our ability to imagine lives outside these norms as holy and blessed. I argue that her method of attending to theological eviction seeks to recognize alterity and is a theology of recognition.

---

1. Sarah, email message to author, June 16, 2014.

Next, I explore and build on Althaus-Reid's indecent theology, which includes her groundbreaking sexual theology of God as queer. The development of a queer God begins by reexamining scenes to which we have already been exposed: scenes of intimacy between primary caregiver and child, between lovers, between subjects as a social group and systems of power/knowledge. Althaus-Reid succinctly states, "In Queer Theology the grounding of the theological reflection lies in human relationships for . . . it is in the scenes of intimacy and the epistemology provided by those excluded from the political heterosexual project in theology that unveilings of God may occur."[2] That is, human experience provides the grounding point for a theology of recognition. Last, I offer critique and implications for subject construction in feminist pastoral theology, utilizing a bi-perspective that is drawn from her scholarship.

## Critiquing "the Poor" of Liberation Theology

Liberation theology arose from repressive social and political contexts in Latin America beginning in the 1960s. Fueled by military regimes and supported by international dollars and arms, whole groups of persons deemed dangerous to the stability of the ruling parties were disappeared, murdered, and tortured. The horrors of this political repression and state terrorism are well-cited: Pinochet's Chile (1973–1990) in which over 40,000 people suffered human rights violations; Salvadoran government repression with 70,000 lives lost in bombing raids and killings waged against civilians in the countryside; and Argentinian state repression and violence during the Dirty War with 30,000 people disappeared or murdered, including both civilian and militant leftists. Religious martyrs also abounded during this time. Well-known martyrs in El Salvador include Archbishop Oscar Romero who was shot (1980); the four churchwomen—Ursuline sister Dorothy Kazel, lay missionary Jean Donovan, and Maryknoll sisters Maura Clark and Ita Ford—who were brutalized and killed (1980); and six Jesuit priests, their housekeeper, and her daughter—Ignacio Ellacuría, Ignacio Martín-Baró, Segundo Montes, Juan Ramón Moreno, Joaquín López y López, Amando López, Elba Ramos, and Celina Ramos—who were murdered at the University of Central America (1989). This horrific state violence and repression, supported by U.S. interventions and policies, backdrop the development of a Marxist

2. Althaus-Reid, *The Queer God*, 114.

inspired liberation theology that uses class analysis as a starting point for attending to the lived realities of subjects. Other theological hallmarks include the development of base ecclesial communities, a theological emphasis on a preferential option for the poor, and a methodological hermeneutic of suspicion toward political and social institutions. Likewise, it is these same hallmarks that Althaus-Reid critiques for reproducing patriarchal norms.

Althaus-Reid's work consistently undermines theological presuppositions that the subjects in need of liberation are able to be liberated through the same set of theological discourses and practices which constructed that subject in the first place. In this section, I offer Marcella Althaus-Reid's practice of writing against liberative discourses that reinscribe the problems they seek to solve: namely through oversimplified narratives by liberationists who interpret the situation to the detriment of those for whom they are speaking in liberation of. For example, Althaus-Reid cites the use of identities that creates non-threatening dialectical categories, such as "the poor," which she argues removes sexuality from discourse. She argues instead for a transgressive theology that challenges the systems that remove "indecent" bodies and lives from the scope of theological reflection. Althaus-Reid shows us how theological discourse, even theological discourse that aims toward liberation, may give a yes, no, or maybe to the questions of subjective recognition. She problematizes who is recognized as "the poor" of liberation theology and attends to other subjects who are misrecognized or not recognized at all in theological discourse.

In an address on a preferential option for the poor to the Faculty of Theology as the University of Montreal in 1994, liberation theologian Gustavo Gutierrez describes what means by "the poor." He writes,

> So what then do we mean by "poor"? I do not think there is any good definition, but we come close to it by saying that the poor are non-persons, the *in-significant*, those who do not count in society and all too often in Christian churches as well. A poor person, for example, is someone who has to wait a week at the door of the hospital to see a doctor. A poor person is someone without social or economic weight, who is robbed by unjust laws; someone who has no way of speaking up or acting to change the situation. Someone who belongs to a despised race and feels culturally marginalized is *in-significant*. In sum, the poor are found in the statistics, but they do not appear there with their own names. We do not know the names of the poor;

they are anonymous and remain so. They are insignificant to
society but not before God.[3]

For Gutierrez, the poor demand the attention of systematic theology
and pastoral practice if theologians and ministers take seriously the gospel's message of liberation. While he identified the namelessness of the
poor, even in places where there is hope to be named and known, such
as church, he does not nuance his description of the poor. For Althaus-
Reid, this description is not only insufficient, but becomes a dialectical
category that calls for analysis.

It is this paradigm of "the poor" as dialectical category that Althaus-
Reid is wary of reiterating. She reminds us that dialectical categories "are
not given, but built."[4] As a built site, "the poor" functions in a heteronormative and patriarchal fashion, removing both gender and sex. As
a result, the dialectical category of "the poor" also removes sexual and
gendered epistemologies. Following from Althaus-Reid, we should ask
Gutierrez to elaborate. Who specifically is waiting a week to see a doctor
and what is the condition from which the subject suffers? What are the
reasons for lack of immediate medical attention? Do ethnicity, gender,
sexual orientation, class, educational attainment, political leanings, or
ability play a role in the waiting? How have these constellations of power
mapped themselves not only on the body of subjects but also on their
psyches and souls? How is the map read by systems of power/knowl-
edge contained within intersubjective, socio-political, and theo-ecclesial
domains?

This line of questioning is consistent with Althaus-Reid's critique
that liberation theology's failure to account for sexuality reifies the poor
as heteronormative subjects of liberation. The complexity of both subjectivity and agency are neutralized in theological discourse. The poor are
made to be objects of pity by appealing to a theologically-based moral
authority, and, at the very same time, the poor are misrecognized or not
recognized at all. For example, there are no poor sex workers in liberation
theology; no transgender dominatrix who experience poverty and insig-
nificance; no gays or bisexuals; and no other perversions which would
risk the continuity of the family and kinship systems nor their participation in economic, social, and political hegemony. Recognition of the
subject in liberation theology is dependent upon a perceived normativity

3. Gutierrez, *Essential Writings*, 145.
4. Althaus-Reid, "The Trouble with Normality," 31.

within the practice of theological and ecclesial discourse. The subject of liberation is thus limited by the kinds of sufferings that the liberation theologian as the agent of interpretation is able to recognize at a personal or social level. Like Butler who reminds us that there are bodies and lives that are rendered invisible by an inability to mourn their deaths, Althaus-Reid argues that failure to hear indecent stories of suffering silences those will not play the part of the deserving poor.

When the poor are misrecognized in liberation theology—that is, depicted as deserving and yet caught in the binds of global forces beyond their individual control, as straight and perhaps coupled with a partner of the opposite anatomy, and often with young, impoverished children—alterity is reduced. As a result, our imaginations are limited in envisioning who God is and what it means to act theologically. Althaus-Reid argues that the reduction of alterity through the creation of dialectical categories like "the poor" are part and parcel of the modern project, a project which imparts a nostalgia for the past. The normative subject of liberation theology is constructed by this nostalgia: poor, God-fearing people come together to resist political and economic oppression.

However, the creation of this nostalgic subject is liberated not through self-will and self-direction, but through the intercessors of liberation or submission to "negotiators of liberation"—priests and theologians—who hegemonically construct the subject of liberation.[5] Thus the subject of liberation theology is constructed from a historical nostalgia, the very one which is made possible by the historical colonization and subsequent religious missions of the conquistador period and forward. As Althaus-Reid writes, "The trouble with normality in Latin America is that it has been constructed by centuries of ideological alliances forged in the history of exploitation of our continent."[6] Thus, renewing the project of liberation theology requires liberating liberation theology from its blindness. In failing to attend to sexuality and gender, liberation theology reproduces the colonial project of domination, marginalization, and exploitation. In other words, without a shift in recognizing subjects made other, misrecognized, and not recognized at all, liberation theology colludes with structural violence and unconsciously participates in harm toward the very subjects who make liberation theology as a discourse and set of theological practices possible.

5. Ibid., 30.
6. Ibid., 26.

## Methods for Liberative Epistemologies

Althaus-Reid's critique of liberation theology leads her to do theology by attending to non-heteronormative bodies. In this next section, I explore her methods to create liberative epistemologies. I argue that her methods aim to recognize subjects who have been denied recognition. Thus she writes a theology of recognition. She does so by attending to those who are evicted from theological discourse. Further, she attends to theological evictions as well as the subaltern in order to locate empowering images of God for the people of God. That is, her theology is not only about theological anthropology, but also doctrines of God and Christology.

In *From Feminist Theology to Indecent Theology*, Althaus-Reid shares with her readers part of her subaltern and indecent narrative as a young, poor person in Argentina. This narrative grounds what I describe as a method of attending to theological evictions:

> I was an adolescent when my family faced eviction. We were given 24 hours to pay overdue rent or leave our house. When the police arrived my mother and myself moved out our few belongings on to the street: some bags of clothes, a box with tea and rice, two chairs. The neighbourhood stood still as if in mourning for yet another eviction; another family put out in the street with a few suitcases and a couple of chairs . . . In times of hyperinflation and liberal economic experiments, my mother and myself ceased to be people. Economic theories became people, evicted us because somehow we became things that did not fit their scheme. The economic system was never evicted; only my mother and myself. As political economic systems evict people so does theology.[7]

In this striking narrative, Althaus-Reid tells us a story in which she parallels physical eviction from her home with theological eviction. Further, I believe she shows us how to begin to think toward a liberative method where the experience of "the poor" is critically asserted and used for epistemology by paying attention to who is evicted from theological discourse. Her (sub)altern narrative—"sub" in parentheses, for by her writing she speaks the subaltern into an altern of resistance—invites those who are not "the poor," including those who inhabit epistemologies of domination, to imagine imperfectly and participate in the world that both shapes her and which she also shapes over time. Her example is

7. Althaus-Reid, *Indecent Theology*, 74.

an example of the ongoing work of recognition between intersubjective subjects as well as subjects and systems, but in a theological register.

What ways of knowing does Althaus-Reid make possible by sharing this pericope? Epistemologically, she critically locates her human experience as a source of theological reflection. First, she centrally locates herself as a neocolonial subject of knowledge. She is a young woman evicted from her home with her mother, and no mention of her father. They gather their few belongings while the neighborhood's silence becomes a mourning song. She is the poor and insignificant that Gutierrez describes. Yet, by her awareness of her existence under these systems of power which map themselves onto her and her narration of them, she resists neocolonial forces. Her narration is an assertion of her very self. In addition, her narration serves as a petitioning for future selves who experience eviction. Second, she narrates how the shackles of domination and submission work in tandem with scheming narratives. Schemes are large scale systematic plans developed and implemented to either obtain some particular object or to put an idea into effect. Schemes dislocate rebellious ideas and resistant subjects, conquering and subjugating both, not by outright force as is assumed in dissections of violence, but by replacing one set of desires with another. At a political level, securing every person's right to have a place to lay one's head was traded for the scheme of national economic freedom and global prosperity. Marcella and her mother were the living human ransom paid for the illusion of theoretical subjects of economy.

Althaus-Reid deploys a methodology which creates sexual and bodily epistemologies. In doing so, she also roots out ideology internal to the production of a supposedly liberative theology by attending to the displaced body. Using sexuality and gender as her lens of analysis, she describes the effects of systematic poverty, liberation theology's blindness to its construction of the normative subject, and social, political, and economic hegemonic regimes that liberation theology and church practices consciously and unconsciously uphold. She leverages her deconstructive theological skill to unveil the process by which theological subjects are made: by disciplining sexuality and relations between the genders; by revealing how systematic theology and morality pronounced by official ecclesial bodies and reveled in by clergy remain (unwitting) supporting forces to neocolonial projects; and by showing how poverty and class analysis cannot be separated from the other forces at work, especially sexism and heterosexism. Her methods reveal the construction

of a hegemonic subject and hegemonic theology that works by manda-
tory theological eviction.

One of Althaus-Reid's major contributions is her observation that
theology evicts poor women who do not do their gender or sex correctly
according to a central ecclesial-moral authority. She argues that the
specific experiences of poor women, when discussed at all, stand as an
addendum to systematic theological constructions.[8] The result is a fixed
subject that is ogled pornographically by a systematic theological gaze.
This gaze cannot be separated from the "characteristics of colonial expansion: bodies are occupied, identities are fixed, women are objectified and
the reflection on God deals more with ideology than with critical reality."[9]
Theological evictions excise those whose experiences may contribute to
a liberative epistemology, and by doing so, objectify the Divine by fixing,
occupying, and ogling the Divine Godhead. Contents of the theological home which will not support theological schemes of social-political
singularity, heteronormativity, and capitalistic desire are cast out: "non-
dualistic patterns of thought, non-hierarchical structures of thought and
alternatives to non-reproductive and repetitive male epistemology."[10]

Liberative epistemologies are made possible by recognizing the
strategies of neocolonial theological evictions as both illusory and real,
and asserting oneself, and one's community, as embodied practices of
resistance and resilience. As in the last chapter, I mean to imply that theological evictions are real illusions. Those who are theologically evicted
experience real injustice. As an illusion, theological evictions are tricks
that are played on those who experience injustice as well as those who
uphold injustice, making us believe that we know what the kin-dom of
God may actually look like. Mirrors reflect mirrors reflect mirrors and
the culminating effect alters our perception of who God is. Further, this
elusive illusion determines what kinds of lives may be brought to the altar of God. One place that Althaus-Reid argues that we might reflect on
theological illusion-building and its consequences for optimal recognition is in the construction of a Latin American Mariology. Along with
Althaus-Reid, I also share my experiences of Mariology.

Theological illusions sustain and mask oppression, and no place is
more ripe for examination than the construction of a Marian liberation

8. Ibid., 75.

9. Ibid., 99.

10. Ibid., 75.

theology. Murals of la Virgen de Guadalupe adorned every other corner in Pilsen and Little Village, two primarily Mexican-American neighborhoods in Chicago. Walking the two blocks from my apartment near Cermak and California to the El, I'd pass by no less than three images—one hidden down an alley, another on a garage door that was rarely open, and another on a very public wall. La Virgen was everywhere, and the first week after I moved in, I was filled with high school memories of learning the story of la Virgen's appearance to Juan Diego, the indigenous peasant. She spoke to him in Nahuatl, and then healed his uncle as a sign of her power. She imprinted herself on his peasant cloak by the inspiration of roses. She is called the Queen of Mexico. Along with my neighbors, I began to pay homage, running my hand over the mural in the alley as I walked through it. As my boxes arrived, I found the scarf imprinted with her image that I had rescued from a give-away pile, and tacked it to the wall of my living room, her body billowing with every opening and shutting of the front door.

There are deep currents which swirl around la Virgen, smoke and mirrors which give way to stasis and containment. Althaus-Reid critiques Mariology for sustaining the confining domestic sphere of feminized *hembrismo*. While *machismo* and patriarchy have elicited comment from socio-political and theological critics, *hembrismo* is a rarely commented upon as an ideology which sustains patriarchy. *Hembrismo* refers to a woman's place in the private sphere. It is a physical, social, and psychological place of containment. A woman goes to her private altar, housed in her bedroom, to light candles and pray for the intercession of God, saints, angels, and especially la Virgen to meet specific needs. As a psycho-social place of containment, Mariology supports women's naïve consciousness. Althaus-Reid argues that instead of seeking means to psychological, social, and economic empowerment, women in Latin America are marked by resignation. They remain outside the masculine territories of paid work, politics, friends, and lovers. Mary as a theological figure of femininity cites the internalization of the Latin American stereotype of the domesticated woman.[11] Mariology as doctrine and theological practice is part of an illusion that sustains a domesticized subject construction. "Mariology," Althaus-Reid writes, "sacralizes and dictates how to be a woman in Latin America, and works as the cornerstone of the feminization of poverty in the continent."[12]

11. Ibid., 31.

12. Ibid.

What ought we do to disassemble the real illusion sustained by a form of liberation theology which misrecognizes and also does not recognize the complex subjectivity of poor women? Althaus-Reid argues that we must examine the scaffolding of theological constructions and question the materials, methods of social production, and the products that arise from the illusions, paying attention to the flow of capital. The materials of the illusory liberation theology are the sources of theological production, sources like systematic theology, Bible, and moral theology. These sources are, in fact, theological capital. They are a certain kind of wealth, and those who possess them, who deftly wield them, turn capital into more capital, while those without access make no headway, further reifying the socio-theological divides between those with proper theological capital and those without. This process results in theological exploitation.

Theological exploitation is an insidious process where some subjects are dominated so that capital gains and theological revenue may increase. That is, the theological thinking that informs neoliberal global economic policies of gain for the elite have also taken root in liberation theology. Althaus-Reid writes, "If the invisible exploited people of theology are women, this happened because the objectification of women in certain sexual and gender status was beneficial to keep the deep sexual principles of theology intact."[13] Mariology and *hembrismo* are examples of this exploitation in action. Exploitation veils itself as progressive development, producing social and theological capital for the common good, but which engenders continued sexual exploitation in church and in society. Althaus-Reid observes, "The point is that in a way Liberation Theology still subordinates itself to patriarchal understandings, which are useful for the purposes of keeping hierarchically-minded ecclesiologies and a systematic theological thinking in accordance with its own rules of importance."[14] In other words, traditional liberation theology unwittingly participates in the making of submissive subjects and then finds itself as Master.

Althaus-Reid suggests taking up a radical theology in order to liberate liberation theology. Going to the root, radical theology emerges from the dirt and dust of those who have found themselves in submissive positions. Radical theology sees that the world is filled with broken things and broken people. Yet brokenness and submission are not the last words

13. Ibid., 76.
14. Ibid., 77.

but providentially become the means for personal, social, and theological transformation. For example, a radical theology might find that God the benevolent father does not measure up to "God La Companera"—an unmarried, sexually fulfilled guerrilla woman who leads her people. Similarly, if liberation theologians were to take up the tasks of a radical theology, orthodoxy might not be reformed but radically displaced and supplanted by new images, new structures, and new thinking and acting.[15]

Thinking radically also helps to disassemble the illusions of magical theological thinking. Crafting God the Father as compassionate liberator cannot do revolutionary work that changes material conditions. Althaus-Reid pointedly notes, "Do god-father images have anything positive? Yes, they may have. Even the slaves in their compounds heard that God the Father was compassionate; that is not a novelty for liberationists."[16] The problem with this doctrine of God is not its intent of liberation and comfort, but its effect. The metaphor of a compassionate God-father is ancient, and the poor are made to fit themselves, their lives, and their identities into this image of God. As theological subjects, the poor are interpellated as naïve and powerless children, reproducing the conditions for domination through colonialism.

A radical, decolonizing theology attentive to those domesticated by heteropatriarchal systems requires an ability to hear assertions that do not fit with Western theological constructions. These assertions may actively fly in the face of the regulatory fictions of church teaching. Experiences of material conditions become internalized oppressions, and subjects are done and undone by the processes of optimal recognition, misrecognition, and non-recognition as they assert themselves. While personal and social suffering, and structural and political violence are real, neocolonization also happens in the act of interpretation, a necessary action for the production of an epistemology. As Althaus-Reid reminds us, the poor, nameless, and insignificant shit the spiritual, while those who would capitalize on their poverty spiritualize their shit.[17] Poor women of all sexual desires, family structures, and anatomical parts are interpellated in such a way that they recognize their own poverty but get no traction from it. While the site of subjectivity of the poor has been

15. Ibid.

16. Ibid., 78.

17. Althaus-Reid, "Feetishism," 135.

used to uphold illusions of examining, caring, and helping in theology and ministry, the illusion flounders when that same site of subjectivity is read as asserting, resisting, subverting, and insurrecting.

While she is critical of liberation theology, Marcella Althaus-Reid also believes that the hopes it contained are still worth working toward. She writes, "Liberation theology must avoid the pitfalls of becoming the remake of the Jesuitical missions, where Latin Americans, especially women, needed to embrace that childlike quality that colonial discourse adores."[18] Liberation theology was indecent for its time. It challenged military regimes and political persecution with acts of love inspired by the gospels.[19] "The first love of the liberationists was for the gospels, but above all, for people and for those whose lives were held in the chains of political and economic oppression," she writes.[20] Like the first generation of Latin American liberation theologians, Althaus-Reid is motivated by this same love. Like her predecessors, she knows that ". . . Latin American liberation theology comes first of all from theological acts of disturbance that are also acts of collective love. Moreover, those acts of love are acts of a subverting, transgressive kind of love."[21] This kind of transgressive love enables her to offer a heterodox theology: an indecent theology made possible by the recognition of the Queer God.

## Bi-Perspectives of an Indecent Theology

Let us come back to Sarah's question: "Does God allow my pining to be all woman?" As I understand her question in light of Marcella Althaus-Reid's theology, which I argue is a theology of recognition, Sarah desires to be recognized by the God given to her through hegemonic, fixing forces. In the eyes of that G/god before whom she comes out of the closet, she will receive a maybe or a no—misrecognition or no recognition at all. The theological system that Sarah experiences casts her and others whose closets are opened as other, sinful, or excluded. As Althaus-Reid notes, "In reality Queer people live lives which are as innocent, more or less, as any other person in this world, but by a process of heterosexual fencing and displacement they have been subjected to a high body theology

18. Althaus-Reid, *Indecent Theology*, 81.
19. Althaus-Reid, "The Trouble with Normality," 22.
20. Ibid.
21. Ibid., 21.

of transgression . . . Queers embody the ultimate trespass in theology."[22] Thinking by way of trespass and transgression is bi-perspective thinking.

Bi-perspective thinking takes account of both the illusion that is created when we read the situation and the emancipatory potential contained within it as well. Social, economic, and theological deviance are liminal sites for an indecent theological method. In two different essays Althaus-Reid bullet-points cues and clues for indecent practices and proposals in theology that have in common their pursuit of the deviant. In the multi-authored collection *Latin America and Liberation Theology*, Althaus-Reid identifies five. First, an indecent theology sees the edges of the construction of the theological subject. Second, it sees the relationship between sexuality and class and traces the ideology that obscures its relationship in liberation theology. Third, it focuses on stories and narratives. Fourth, it reads the Bible and religious traditions, including Christianity, sexually. Last, it explores themes and metaphors beyond heterosexuality.[23]

In "On Wearing Skirts without Underwear: Poor Women Contesting Christ," Althaus-Reid proposes a similar hermeneutic of suspicion. She identifies four hermeneutical threads that share a sexual trajectory that impacts the interpretation and construction of the subject. She writes that an indecent hermeneutic must seek "a more realistic, non-androcentric anthropology, where women are in control of their desires and pleasures, and in complete freedom to express themselves sexually with their own bodies, with other women, with men or both."[24] Secondly, in light of new theological anthropologies, spiritual and economic matters must be recast. Thirdly, liberation continues as a task, but is hermeneutically recast in such a way that the indecent subjects of liberation theology are also agents. For example, recasting the female sexual victim into agent requires changing the focus of conversation partners to include female sexual researchers. Last, an indecent theology also points to the difference between love and sexuality, disentangling the suffering created by theological conflation of the two.[25]

An indecent theology is concerned with process and content, form and function, and the linkages between the two. An indecent theology

22. Althaus-Reid, *The Queer God*, 169.

23. Althaus-Reid, "The Trouble with Normality," 35.

24. Althaus-Reid, *Indecent Theology*, 88.

25. Ibid.

knows that inattention to sexuality and gender in liberation theology—a methodological matter—results in limited content and the maintenance of theologies which do not liberate. As such, suspicion of class ideology cannot stand alone. Rather, suspicion of sex/gender systems is also vital to identifying and deconstructing the ideological paradigms which fix people. For example, she argues that heterosexuality and its reification of normative kinship systems produces subjects fit for exploitation. Exploitation cannot proceed without the help of theological systems that uphold the God-given permanence of a certain idea of the family. She explains,

> Concretely, heterosexuality is also an ideological construction that reifies people in even more profound ways than class. At least we can say that heterosexuality as an ideology is not politically innocent or economically naïve. Its way of conceiving and organizing both families and societies has ramifications for larger issues such as the destruction of the environment and the colonial/neocolonial way of understanding life through expansion, destruction, profit, and exploitation.[26]

While attending to sex/gender systems in liberation theology remains of prime importance to Althaus-Reid's project, she also asks us to pay attention to that which is cast as deviant as a methodological matter. Attention to sex/gender deviance is means for liberation theology to identify alternative, liberative, and transformative practices and theories. She writes, "Indecenting as a hermeneutical circle is in a way a call to deviancy from centers of knowledge and faith to the margins, without returning to the center. It is an attempt to claim the marginal knowledge of God as a foundation for an alternative theological praxis of liberation."[27]

Althaus-Reid argues that practicing liberation theology in a register of sex/gender deviance moves us toward justice, toward holiness, toward transcendence by a materially oriented theology, and ultimately toward a God who disrobes, exposing God's very self. What might recognition of this God mean for pastoral theological constructions of subjectivity as well as practice? Althaus-Reid urges us to rethink the geographies of holiness, to ascertain from which analyses, theologies, practices, and ways of being and thinking bodies have been disappeared. Practicing recognition in these contexts may lead to both loving and unpleasant encounters and

26. Althaus-Reid, "The Trouble with Normality," 27.
27. Ibid.

critiques as those who have been theologically subjugated assert their being and becoming. As Althaus-Reid reminds us, queer spirituality "can
claim that God the Stranger amongst our community of strangers may
have declared us, made us, irredeemably lost in the eyes of the church
and Christian ethics, yet it is not we who are lost."[28]

## Critiques and Implications for Feminist Pastoral Theology

Reading Marcella Althaus-Reid's corpus requires both stamina and wit.
She calls her writing "a theology of camp self-disclosure," but this description does not adequately capture her astute theological reflections
lodged in continental philosophy, liberation theology, and embodiment.[29] Nor does it reflect her courage in writing. Following her death
in 2009, postcolonial theologian Kwok Pui-Lan remarked, "By shatter-
ing all taboos and laying out her truths with such tenacity, she offered
us by example the fierce battle for truth and for freedom of thought."[30]
Natalie K. Watson observed, "Marcella Althaus-Reid will be remembered
as someone who took theology where good Christian theologians fear
to tread."[31] Her writing, while not systematic, is nonetheless significant.
Mayra Rivera Rivera comments, Althaus-Reid "practices alternative
modes of representation. The multiple body images in her texts do not
add up to an organized, whole, unified body – or to a systematic theory of
embodiment—but they do produce aesthetic effects that are theologically
significant."[32]

Most significant is Althaus-Reid's sustained attention to sexuality
and sensuality which also cause discomfort to her readers. When Althaus-
Reid describes the musky scent of a lemon seller, Rivera reveals that the
"unexpected sensual excess perturbs me . . . as if the text has reached out
(and touched me!)".[33] Regarding that same self-revelatory story, womanist Emilie M. Townes comments, "I read about these women and was
made immediately uncomfortable and angry. I was being cast into the

---

28. Ibid., 165.

29. Althaus-Reid, "On Non-Docility and Indecent Theologians," 182.

30. Pui-Lan, "Body and Pleasure in Postcoloniality," 32.

31. Watson, "Uncloseting the Divine," 191.

32. Rivera, "Corporeal Visions and Apparitions," 82.

33. Ibid., 79.

unwanted role of the voyeur—unintentionally, but deliberately."[34] As a sexual theologian, Althaus-Reid's work calls into question the assumption that sexual theology is an addendum to proper theology. Sexual theology shatters the assumption of proper theology by arguing that we must address lust, desire, love, fantasy, and experience whenever we conceptualize any theological project. Kwok Pui-Lan explains, "Sexual theology is not just the specific concern of queer, gay, lesbian, bisexual and trangendered theologians—as it is often assumed to be—but a project that all theologians, whether consciously or unconsciously, participate in."[35]

Althaus-Reid's observations raise critical questions for feminist pastoral theology. How ought a discipline originating in attention to women's experiences of suffering and fulfillment attend more fully to sexuality when offering accounts of subjectivity? What epistemologies are foreclosed and unknown which we have not yet mourned, and what are the consequences of that? What schemes are we baited to naturalize through our discipline? What rebellious ideas and resistant subjects are dislocated, and subsequently evicted, through economies, social-political structures, and theological epistemologies?

When I read with Althaus-Reid as a companion, my assumptions about the production of knowledge are called into question, and as such I must consider what thinking from a bi-perspective brings to pastoral theology. For example, in the ethnography *Death Without Weeping: The Violence of Everyday Life in Brazil*, anthropologist Nancy Scheper-Hughes investigates the social production of indifference to child death. As a community health worker focused on child and maternal health in Alto do Cruzeiro, a shantytown in the northeastern state of Pernambuco, Scheper-Hughes chronicles her first encounter with child death. A young mother brought her very sick male baby to Scheper-Hughes, who took him to the hospital. Despite her efforts and those of other medical professionals, the baby died. Scheper-Hughes writes that she was both overwhelmed with grief and fearful of the reaction of the mother. Carrying the dead weight in her arms through the shantytown while weeping bitter tears, she was confused when the mother took the baby from her arms in an unconcerned manner. Scheper-Hughes writes,

34. Townes, "Marcella Althaus-Reid's *Indecent Theology*," 63.
35. Pui-Lan, "Theology as a Sexual Act," 151.

> Noting my red eyes and tear-stained face, the woman turned
> to comment to a neighbor woman standing by, "*Hein, hein, co-*
> *itada! Engraçada, não é*; Tsk! Tsk! Poor thing! Funny isn't she?"
> What was funny or amusing seemed to be my inappropriate
> display of grief and my concern over a matter of so little conse-
> quence. No one, least of all the mothers, had expected the little
> tyke to live in any case.[36]

From Scheper-Hughes' perspective, the idea of the casual acceptance of child death is cognitively perplexing and emotionally jarring.
She argues that indifference to child death is not merely a cultural difference to be tolerated or respected. Instead, indifference of this kind is
born of the routinization exhibited in the lives of individuals, and un-
critically reproduced through formal, public institutions and located in
social practices. She specifically cites the loss of breast-feeding culture
as a matter of somatic scarcity and its replacement with formula made
by multinational corporation Nestlé; poverty and its effects on mortality
and fertility patterns; and an aversion to medical abortions and unnatural
forms of birth control, such as the pill and condoms, coupled with strong
religious sentiments linking prematurely terminated pregnancies with
sin.[37]

While the mother Scheper-Hughes describes may be routinized to
indifference, keeping in mind Althaus-Reid's critiques leads to alternative
readings of the feminist subject. When I first read this story, I placed
the unnamed mother in the dialectical category of the poor. Along with
Scheper-Hughes, I was concerned about the inappropriate emotional response and as such read this story in the modality of a tragedy. However,
reading with Althaus-Reid, we must ask how feminist pastoral theologians might respond as we consider the subject's formation and theorize
from it. Along with liberation theology, pastoral theology mourns both
child death and an emotional response which lacks grief. However, we
must ask what her tsk-tsking means, knowing that this affects how we
understand her subjectivity and the form of care to offer. It is here that
Althaus-Reid informs how we might think from an indecent theological
method and bi-perspective. From an indecent theological method, we
might consider our nameless woman as not only subject but also agent.
Contained within her tsk-tsking is both indifference and resistance. We
lack sufficient information, but we can imagine various situations which

36. Scheper-Hughes, *Death Without Weeping*, 271.

37. Ibid., 316–17, 327, 333.

may have preceded the short narrative that Scheper-Hughes provides. For the sake of thinking from a bi-perspective, let us play with the idea that non-consensual sex resulted in pregnancy. Steeling one's emotions is indicative of both trauma and a desire to resist death-dealing forces. If this was the case, then Scheper-Hughes essentially misrecognizes her subject. By examining Scheper-Hughes response, we inventory the traces of a scholarly production which, while intending to be liberative, may further colonize the nameless Brazilian woman. A colonizing scholarly production reinforces subjugation of not only the unnamed mother. In Scheper-Hughes, as elsewhere, a nameless woman whose motives, life, and desires are unknown, is subject to misrecognition. She is stripped of her agency. Additionally, the researcher who cares about relational and material poverty is also caught in dominating patterns of thinking because of her mode of intersubjective address. Can we hear "tsk tsk" as an assertion that calls for a different theological response rather than only a confirmation of the subject's socially produced indifference that comes as a result of the structural violence of poverty? Can we read violence in the epistemology between knowing subject and known subject? As a pastoral theologian, I, like Rivera and Townes, am made to feel uncomfortable in thinking this way. Perhaps, this is precisely the point.

Althaus-Reid challenges feminist pastoral theologians to recognize sexuality as a category that exceeds identity. Sexuality is not merely a category to consider for justice-oriented pastoral theology and care. Rather, attending to sexuality throughout the discourse of feminist pastoral theology may create new ways of offering care—an indecent care. Following from Althaus-Reid, indecent care is marked by an attention to sexuality at multiple intersections in order to reveal how subjects are recognized, misrecognized, or not recognized at all in theological systems. Reflecting on subjectivity through the lens of indecency and the non-heteronormative body in light of critical social and political systems broadens the foundation of feminist pastoral theological anthropology. Specifically, by dialoguing with Althaus-Reid and framing her work as reflecting on recognition, I believe that feminist pastoral theology can more adequately attend to nagging questions of how to account for social injustice as we care for individuals.

In the preceding three chapters, I introduced theories of recognition offered by Benjamin, Butler, and Althaus-Reid, and outlined the implications of their thought for feminist pastoral theology. In the next three chapters, I reflect on the implications and develop constructive proposals for feminist pastoral theology. In the next chapter, I describe how recognizing social and political injustices is critical to subject construction and to pastoral praxis.

# 6

## *Recognizing Injustice*

In the preceding chapters, I described the problem and solution of recognition from intersubjective, social-political, and theological frameworks. I noted that though delineated as distinct areas, we should see these frameworks informing each other and the subject. Theological precepts inform the ways that we subjects understand ourselves, our agency, and God. Intersubjective relationships and family life shape us in our perceptions of the world. Social-political life shapes our identity, and interpellates our experiences and self-perceptions. We risk misunderstanding the complex relationship between subjectivity, personal suffering, and social injustice when categories organized because of our desire to care and act justly have us misperceive, extrapolate, or leave behind marginalized and subjugated peoples as we theologize.

   Giving accounts of ourselves, and inviting other selves to give their accounts, requires a critical lens attentive not only to the telling of a life as a set of events or through identity alone, but the telling of a life through a paradigm that reads emotional currents for what is said, what is not said, and what might never be sayable.[1] Personal and social suffering, structural violence, and political repression wear on selves-in-relation. We can become distant from ourselves and our loves. Continued experiences of

---

1. Froehle et al., "Complex Identities," 20. This triple concept of the said, unsaid, and the unsayable follows from sociologist Pierre Bourdieu in his *Outline of a Theory of Practice.*

social injustice and personal suffering may dislocate us from the selves-in-relation that we most desire. We lay aside our greatest hopes for mutual recognition, love, and personal and social transformation, and instead hope for survival or submit to death. It is for this reason that pastoral theologians are called to the tasks of empowering, liberating, resisting, and inciting as forms of care which foster healing and wholeness.

What are tools that feminist pastoral theologians have to wield for the flourishing of all God's people? I argue that enacting a care that does justice requires the capacity to lament and to confront. Further, feminist pastoral theologian's familiarity with the affective landscape of human life enables these capacities. In this chapter, I proceed by attending to structural violence, first, and then political repression, to describe how they affect subject formation. In doing so, I also describe the difficulties we encounter as we actively seek to recognize othered subjects who are misrecognized or not recognized at all. I conclude that cultivating the capacity for lamentation and confrontation creates conditions that build toward resilient selves-in-relation. Building toward resilient selves-in-relation is a pastoral task oriented toward just care, and ultimately, human flourishing.

## Structural Violence and Subject Formation

Suffering happens everyday, and so does violence. But what counts as violence? Obviously, we know certain one-time and on-going actions are violent: terrorism and bombings, rape, crimes, murders, and wars. We can observe this violence. We will often say that "we know it when we see it." Behind each of these of these violent actions is an actor. Thus, as philosopher and cultural theorist Slavoj Žižek reminds us, violence with an agent or actor is subjective violence.[2] There is a subject who acts to do harm.

Žižek presents two additional types of violence that he groups as objective violence. Objective violence has no actor or agent behind them. He names them as symbolic violence and systemic violence. Symbolic violence is found in language where patterns of social domination and claims of universalism are habitually reproduced in speech. Systemic violence is the "catastrophic consequences of the smooth functioning of

---

2. Žižek, *Violence*, 2.

our economic and political systems."[3] Both types of objective violence are often invisible. We mistake symbolic and systemic violence for the normal state of affairs, the even keel against which we judge subjective violence as the deviation from the norm.

However, there is a more insidious kind of violence which is structural in nature. Expanding Žižek's category of systemic violence, I prefer the use of the term structural violence because it describes the limiting of human agency and the confluence of structures, like institutions, laws, and environments, which impede human flourishing. Structural violence is objective, meaning that there is no one agent, actor, or author behind the violent acts that cause social suffering, but which become evident at the individual level. Medical anthropologist and physician Paul Farmer argues that social suffering is "structured by historically given (and often economically driven) processes and forces that conspire . . . to constrain agency."[4] Consent to submit is not given; instead "life choices are structured by racism, sexism, political violence, *and* grinding poverty."[5] One does not submit to the extremes of this violence and suffering, but instead comes to exist in these systems. Passivity is construed as a yes when in fact no process for assertion or conferral of recognition has occurred. As a result, one's agency is limited.

It helps to hear an account of a life lived in light of structural violence. Paul Farmer tells the story of Acéphie whose story is not unique. A poor, young Haitian woman from a rural area, she contracts HIV from a sexual liaison with a married soldier, the only men who receive a regular salary in the area. She moves to Port-au-Prince to find a *moun prensipal*, an unmarried main man, and works as a maid for $30 a month. She finds her main man, Blanco, and becomes pregnant before they marry. She is fired because of her pregnancy. Her fiancée calls off the engagement. She returns to her rural village to have the baby and soon after the birth her HIV positive status becomes visible, devastating her body and spirit until she dies.[6]

I recognize that I have told Acéphie's story without nuance, without her voice, and in a way which may misrecognize her. Yet, this is the closest that I can come given the constraints that also distance me from Acéphie.

3. Ibid.
4. Farmer, "On Suffering and Structural Violence," 263.
5. Ibid.
6. Ibid., 266–67.

In using Acéphie, I echo Farmer's point that Acéphie's story is not just a personal tale of victimization or another citation of tragic individual suffering. Nor is it unique. Her story is indicative of a network of suffering across the globe that women, children, people of color, and those who do not live their lives according to heteronormative constraints face. With limited agency and under less than ideal conditions, Acephie responds. Violence structures and impinges upon her capacity for self-growth. What are the obligations that Western, educated feminist pastoral theologians have to Acephie if we are, indeed, selves-in-relation? Are there frameworks which advance social justice while caring personally?

A capabilities approach is a starting point. Economist Amartya Sen and philosopher Martha Nussbaum are two theorists of global justice who utilize a capabilities approach to respond to the shape of structural violence. The capabilities approach argues that justice is advanced when people have the capability to pursue the ends they desire. As such, freedoms to pursue those ends are required. This is a significant shift from thinking about poverty as economic misdistribution to thinking about poverty as capability deprivation. Nussbaum states that a capabilities approach to justice pivots on the "idea that all human beings have an inherent dignity and what they require is life circumstances that are worthy of that dignity."[7] Or, as Sen articulates, a just society requires that individuals have "substantive freedoms—the capabilities—to choose a life one has reason to value."[8] As such, a capabilities approach supports systems which diminish poverty, such as access to consistent health care and basic education for a nation's citizens.

Acephie's identity as a Haitian and as a woman certainly play roles in our understanding of her suffering, but her story cannot be considered without conscious reflection on the effects of structural violence on the psyche. Beyond limited opportunities to develop her economic capabilities, structural violence wears on those who suffer in such a way that on-going trauma becomes tedious and numbing, both to those who experience it and to those who witness it. Trauma need not always originate in a massive, one-time event. Rather, micro-traumas are cumulative, forming, deforming, and reforming the self-in-relation. Speaking about Acéphie's story and the stories of his other poor, female patients, Farmer comments,

7. Nussbaum, "Justice," 124.
8. Sen, *Development as Freedom,* 74.

There is a deadly monotony in their stories: young women—or teenaged girls—who were driven to Port-au-Prince by the lure of an escape from the harshest poverty; once in the city, each worked as a domestic; none managed to find financial security. The women interviewed were straightforward about the nonvoluntary aspect of their sexual activity: in their opinions, they had been driven into unfavorable unions by poverty. Indeed, such testimony should call into question facile notions of "consensual sex."[9]

Pastoral theologians, caring ministers, and social justice practitioners are witnesses who seek to ensure that the violence of suffering through structures is heard and interpreted as oppressive, even if there is no one dominator. It is an illusion to understand Acéphie's choices as willing participation or even unconscious consent. Too often cooptation into systems which subjugate is misinterpreted as tacit consent in persons who experience the monotony of everyday social suffering. Over time, subjugation under the colonizing, capitalist, heteropatriarchal systems of domination produces the social indifference lived out in the context of particular lives.

However, describing structural violence is tricky. It resists telling in a linear method where the casualties and causalities are easily visible. Structural violence is masked by complex and hard to predict natural, social, and political forces. Take, for example, the 7.0 earthquake in Haiti on January 12, 2010. It devastated the country, the poorest nation in the Western hemisphere, and especially the capital city of Port-au-Prince, with an estimation of over 222,570 dead, 300,572 injured, and 2.3 million, a quarter of the population, displaced.[10] Coverage of the natural disaster was extensive. It would be hard to believe that a significant population of the world's human inhabitants are unaware of this social suffering, caused by non-agential environmental factors, but amplified through grinding poverty, lack of national infrastructure, and political instability as a democracy. However, what became less visible were the harms reproduced through ongoing structural causes of suffering.

Nearly ten months after the earthquake, a bacterial strain of cholera found in South Asia appeared in Haiti. Haitians has not been exposed to cholera in roughly a century, so with such little resistance, 4,500 died and

9. Farmer, "On Suffering and Structural Violence," 271.
10. Fisher, *Haiti*, 3.

300,000 were sickened.[11] An independent panel of experts from across the globe assembled to determine how cholera was introduced into the Haitian environs. They considered three hypotheses: first, that the strain was introduced to Haiti via the Gulf of Mexico after the tectonic plates shifted; second, that the strain was already present in Haiti before the earthquake but evolved into a pathogenic strain; or third, that a human host inadvertently carried the strain into Haiti. Haitian locals particularly believed the third hypothesis, arguing that UN soldiers from a country with cholera introduced the strain while serving at the MINUSTAH (Mission de Nations Unies pour la Stabilisation en Haïti) camp. The panel confirmed that the bacterial strain of *Vibrio cholerae* was unintentionally introduced by a human carrier and transmitted through fecal matter in the Meye Tributary System of the Artibonite River. The widespread contamination, though, resulted from several factors beyond the control of any one individual. They write,

> This explosive spread was due to several factors, including the widespread use of river water for washing, bathing, drinking, and recreation; regular exposure of agricultural workers to irrigation water from the Artibonite River; the salinity gradient in the Artibonite River Delta, which provided optimal environmental conditions for rapid proliferation of *Vibrio cholerae*; the lack of immunity of the Haitian population to cholera; the poor water and sanitation conditions in Haiti; the migration of infected individuals to home communities and treatment centers; the fact that the South Asian type *Vibrio cholerae* strain that caused the outbreak causes a more severe diarrhea due to the larger production of the more potent classical type of cholera toxin; and, the conditions in which cholera patients were initially treated in medical facilities did not prevent the spread of the disease to other patients or to the health workers.[12]

The panel concluded that all these factors created another instance of social suffering created by the confluence of circumstances. They assert that the outbreak "was not the fault of, or deliberate action of, a group or individual."[13] Here, oppressive forces have no particular agent, perpetrator, or dominator against whom one can assert one's self. Instead, all subjects are affected by ongoing structural violence.

11. Cravioto, et al., *Cholera*, 3.

12. Ibid., 4.

13. Ibid., 29.

As described by Jessica Benjamin, the intersubjective imperative to reestablish the tension between recognition and assertion simply does not work here. Indeed, to call for recognition between two subjects misses the fact that even good intentions may cause harm, such as the human carrier of *Vibrio cholerae* who entered Haiti in an effort to assist in disaster efforts. This line of argumentation is advanced by John L. McKnight, Professor of Education and Social Policy at Northwestern University. In *The Careless Society: Community and Its Counterfeits*, McKnight identifies the "professional problem" of care as a major contributor to cycles of poverty and oppression. In interviews conducted through asset-based community development, the poor and advocates for the poor described their victimization: as "poor people defined as deficient by those whose incomes depend upon the deficiency they define."[14] Building on philosopher, Catholic priest, and social critic Ivan Illich's work in *Medical Nemesis* (1982), McKnight argues the professional problem is best explained through the iatrogenic argument—that the work of helpers and carers actually hurts and disables those they assist with "sick-producing medicine, stupidifying education, and criminalizing justice."[15] In these cases, as is the case of the cholera outbreak, the unpredictability of social suffering creates conditions that further exile selves-in-relation from self-determining community, impairing intersubjective, social, and theological recognition.

## Political Repression and Subject Formation

As I mentioned in the case of Haiti, an individual's experience of social suffering cannot be separated from collective experiences of political repression that are subjectively and objectively violent. Liberation psychologist Ignacio Martín-Baró, a Spanish Roman Catholic priest and one of the six Jesuits murdered by a Salvadoran death squad on November 16, 1989, provided intellectual acuity on these topics and the necessity of a political psychology to confront, document, and analyze political regimes that oppress *the people*—a concept he argues that can be defined by historical particularity, political solidarity, and socioeconomic exploitation. He explains, "*The people* is a search and an effort directed at creating a concrete community of free people. *The people* is . . . a denial of all

14. McKnight, *The Careless Society*, 19.
15. Ibid, 20.

slavery, not as an achieved present reality, but as a dynamic demand, as a vocation—a calling."[16] The dynamic demands are the petitions and assertions of selves-in-relation who exercise their "communitarian vocation."[17]

When petitions and assertions are vocalized by communities, established political powers act in violence in order to repress and silence. Even more insidiously, the communitarian vocation to freedom "can remain trapped in the unconscious, repressed by the jealous violence of the oppressor."[18] When we begin to analyze how subjects give accounts of themselves, we must take seriously that political repression is used as a tool to denigrate and destroy selves-in-relation. For this reason, it is helpful to read the essay "The Psychological Value of Political Repression" by Martín-Baró. In this essay he cites the effects of repressive violence on the psyche of the repressor, the repressed, and the spectator.

Repressors, those who carry out violent acts, experience two psychological effects. First, they internalize another's dehumanization in response to cognitive dissonance between violence and other principles, like democratic or religious values. Second, they act out learned habits of violence to resolve interpersonal conflicts.[19] Repressors undergo psychic splits, positing their social group of us and we as "the good" over and against opposing groups of them as "the bad."[20] In his context, this occurs along the fault line of ethnic identity in Central and South America, where indigenous peoples are repressed economically, socially, and politically. Repression is felt as the lack of social collaboration, the lack of effective and transparent communication, and the enacting of repressive cycles of violence.

Because political repression is often directed against basic human needs such as food, shelter, and work, and because repression punishes behavior without providing an alternative to learned behaviors, the repressed experience the routinization of their lives, like that of Acephie or the Brazilian mother who laughed at Scheper-Hughes. They internalize a passivity to their own lives. Martín-Baró comments that is not uncommon to hear those in the campo say, "It is better to die fast from a bullet

16. Martín-Baró, *Writings for a Liberation Psychology*, 182.

17. Ibid.

18. Ibid.

19. Ibid., 156–57.

20. Ibid., 166.

than slowly from hunger."[21] Personal passivity congeals into political passivity. Repressive violence discourages behaviors through fear. The repressed internalize emotions that they associate when they encounter the regime—police, army, government—and thus are inhibited from action against the regime. Rules of the authority figure are internalized as inhibitions and lead to guilt when evaluative criterion of correct behavior is violated. Internalized guilt leads to a desire to hide transgressions. Consequently, the repressed also experience aggression as a result of their frustration.

Spectators of violent repression experience psychological effects that are dependent upon their identification with the repressed. If they identify with the repressors, the spectator may scapegoat the victims, separating themselves from those who deserved punishment, and distancing themselves from "guerrillas," "subversives," or "criminal" elements. Those who identify with the repressed may experience cognitive dissonance as they name the repressors—"fascist," "murderer," etc.[22] The most important psychological effect for the spectator is the learned value of violent power in response to social situations. Martín-Baró writes, "The daily spectacle of violence committed by repressive forces teaches and encourages spectators to use similar behaviors to solve their own problems."[23] Spectators observe, and then become repressors in their own right.

Political repression limits agency and multiplies social suffering by dismantling any form of consent. Here, submission is required for existence. Individual assertions against the regime guarantee a protracted death from starvation, the purgatory of torture, or the anxiety of anticipating an attack against oneself or one's closest friends and family. As an aspect of structural violence, political repression challenges us to understand subject formation in political contexts where the assertion that petitions for recognition is met with violence to the body and the psyche.

What are the means that selves-in-relation possess to confront political repression and subjugation by fear? The Cochabamba water revolt in 2000 is one example of how cultural identity, although repressed, can still give rise to resistance in the face of oppressive forces. Before releasing funds to support water services, World Bank officials demanded privatization, and water rights were sold by the Bolivian government to Bechtel

21. Ibid., 160.
22. Ibid., 164.
23. Ibid.

Enterprises, one of the largest corporations in the world. The people of Cochabamba and surrounding environs, many of whom are Quechuan, took to the streets to protest. An iconic photograph captures the spirit of communitarian vocation: a Bolivian woman in traditional dress and plaited hair stands on a downtown street in Cochabamba. A single rock slingshot uncoils from her left hand as a militarized line of men approach. Her body and her person on the line, facing down government forces, she pivots for momentum, her singular action emblematic of a community demanding recognition for self- and communal-determination.[24]

Additionally, organization and recognition of social identities is a key leverage point for political representation which can resist political repression. For example, on January 22, 2006, the indigenous people of Bolivia, who make up nearly sixty five percent of the population, celebrated a significant win for their social recognition and political representation when Evo Morales, an Amayran Indian coca grower and union leader from the Chapare region, was sworn in as the first indigenous president. Wearing a jacket embroidered with traditional Andean designs, Morales asked for a moment of silence for the fallen heroes of the Bolivian rebellion, and then recounted in a booming voice how the indigenous peoples were subjugated for the past 500 years. He critiqued the capitalist and colonial systems that had looted the natural resources of Bolivia and the political leaders who had aligned their policies with those demanded by the International Monetary Fund's neoliberal policies, resulting in the oppression and economic exploitation of the indigenous peoples. Staring down former presidents, Morales announced that his government had come to power to change the historical situation of the indigenous people and put an end to the colonial state.[25] Since 2006, he has become even more beloved by the people. On January 21, 2015, the people gathered at the ruins of Tiwanaku for his 3rd swearing in as President of the Plurinational State of Bolivia. At this holy site, leaders of indigenous communities initiated Morales as leader and visionary for the people. With words as weapons, and not just rocks of rebellion, the people of Bolivia asserted again their capacity for self- and communal-determination through social recognition.

24. Schultz, "The Cochabamba Water Revolt and Its Aftermath," 8–9.
25. Gómez, "Evo Morales Turns the Tide of History," 140–45.

## To Lament

Therefore I will not restrain my mouth;
I will speak in the anguish of my spirit;
I will complain in the bitterness of my soul . . .
When I say, 'My bed will comfort me,
my couch will ease my complaint,'
then you scare me with dreams
and terrify me with visions,
so that I would choose strangling
and death rather than this body.
I loathe my life; I would not live forever.
Let me alone, for my days are a breath.[26]

The words of Job, written between the sixth century and the fourth century BCE, are not so far removed from words of those who experience submission and domination in personal relationships, structural violence, or political repression. Like the author, they (and we) may be persecuted by another person or entity which leaves them loathing their lives. However, unlike the author, domination sometimes means that the person who suffers does not cry out in anguish, does not wail lament, does not complain in the bitterness of her soul. Instead, the on-going trauma of violence is normalized so that the subject is either muted, for example the slave who thinks nothing of fetching glasses or opening the door for his master, or responds in a way that seems contradictory to the emotion presented as in the case of the Brazilian woman who laughed at Scheper-Hughes's tears.

Social theorists of emotion have argued that the emotive aspects of the self are shaped in relationship to culture.[27] For example, in Japan anger is an inappropriate emotion to express between two persons of the same social groups. In contrast, in the United States anger between individuals who are colleagues or friends is acceptable.[28] Emotions, then, are not "innate or prior to social engagement," but instead are "cultural

---

26. Job 7:11, 13–16.
27. Harré and Parrott, *The Emotions*, 1.
28. Oatley et al., *Understanding the Emotions*, 64.

artifacts" built from social norms, interpersonal relationships, and cultural structures.[29] Pastoral theologian Barbara J. McClure explains,

> . . . our sociocultural contexts encourage the cultivation of certain dispositions and not others. As we develop and mature we learn what actions and emotions are appropriate in what contexts. The relations of communication and culture in which emotional vocabularies and moral regulations develop are figurations of power balances that change by context and with history.[30]

In other words, the muted emotions of the person who submits, or cultivated indifference to the brutality of life, are conditioned emotions that stem from the cycles of submission and domination to oppressive persons and systems. Structural violence and political repression then also form subjects through fear and aggression, and subjects are then limited in their capability to assert themselves in social and political spheres. What, then, is an appropriate pastoral theological response?

While culture in the form of social location, personal relationships, and structural violence may shape the range of emotions available to those who suffer, it is not merely cultural. Relationships of care, whether by social or ecclesial institutions, the political state, or primary caretakers, may be unjust and oppressive. As a feminist pastoral theologian, I believe that we must critique the insidious everyday violence that makes a subject's ability to wail in lament personally difficult or even incomprehensible. When persons who experience everyday violence and social suffering cannot lament for themselves in a way that is broadly recognizable, pastoral theologians and caregivers are called to stand against oppression and injustice by offering their lamentation as a form of solidarity and resistance to deformation of the subject.

To be in solidarity extends beyond compassion and empathy for others. To be in solidarity requires a commitment to be in the struggle—en la lucha[31]—with those who experience oppression and domination.[32] Pastoral theologians and caregivers, indeed all of creation, are called to be moved, emotionally, relationally, and even physically by the virtue of mercy when confronting injustices. Pastoral theologian Brita L. Gill-Aus-

---

29. McClure, *Moving Beyond Individualism*, 197.

30. Ibid.

31. Isasi-Díaz, *En la Lucha/In the Struggle*, 1.

32. Gill-Austern, "Engaging Diversity and Diference," 35.

tern asserts, "We must struggle alongside of the suffering in the pursuit of justice-making, knowing that by being in closer proximity relationally and physically more may be asked of us than we had anticipated."[33]

Lament is one aspect of *the more* required of us as relational beings who are both agents and subjects in the projects of becoming ourselves. Without lament as a Christian pathos, we are ill-equipped to encounter and counter domination, oppression, and suffering. Instead, we are stuck in "silent despair," "forgotten sadness," and "frozen grief."[34] We become comfortably numb to ourselves and to the pain of others that calls for a response. Lament is grief work. It is the voice that cries out, like Job's. Even when those who suffer injustices cannot cry out, lament offered by those in solidarity is an assertion that calls for recognition. It is a distinctively recognition-oriented response that lays the groundwork for further engagement through resilient performances and hopeful participations. When communities of faith, pastoral theologians, and caregivers lament, we acknowledge that we are selves-in-relation who are not only subject to domination, structural violence, or political repression, but also agents whose voices ought to rise resiliently in the face of the systems that cause suffering. Further, lamenting in solidarity ensures that theology and politics are not marked off as separate containers of belief and action, but instead bleed into each other, cutting through hearts of stone.

When we wail our lament, we affirm the human need and ability to heal from political and social wrongs that cause undue social suffering and oppression. Writing about South African apartheid, feminist practical theologian Denise M. Ackermann observes that the systems of repression "required compliant interlocking political, social and religious systems."[35] Thus, she argues, social healing cannot be separated from political healing. As a form of political repression, apartheid psychologically harmed all those subject to it. Thus, victims and perpetrators need the opportunity to lament wrong-doing and the loss of humanity in order to heal from social and political oppression. Lament then becomes a theological and political act of assertion. It is also an embodied act of resistance to the status quo. For example, Ackermann describes "keening bodies" of women who are deemed liturgically inappropriate in South Africa's mainline Christian churches, yet who publicly lament for days

33. Ibid, 36.
34. Blain-Wallace, "The Politics of Tears," 184.
35. Ackermann, "A Voice Was Heard in Ramah," 81.

on end in African rural villages and townships.[36] The keening body of an African woman is a formidable site; her cries affirm that not all is right; there are wrongs that must be acknowledged. Lament is the cry of resistance against being turned in a symbol of the subjugated Other.

In Garhwal, India, in the Central Himalayas, the Harijans are the lowest castes of persons. They suffer economically, physically, politically, and even spiritually. They are constantly humiliated, with insults hurled at them, or addressed as boy or girl, the form of "you" reserved for animals and children. As anthropologist William S. Sax writes, "If ever there was a 'community of suffering,' this is it."[37] In the face of their suffering, they too lament, crying out to the Hindu deity Bhairav. Bhairav is their god of justice who responds when the Harijan call out, "I have no one." Commenting on the hidden transcripts that detail Bhairav's appearance, the secreted property of the Harijan, Sax explains, "When the protagonist utters this sentence, it is a moment of maximum weakness and helplessness, and yet it is at precisely this moment that the god of justice appears, to punish the wicked and bring justice to the oppressed."[38]

In rituals the Harijan call on Bhairav and ask him to manifest himself in the bodies of the believers. Gathered together they sing songs and proclaim "I have no one," a profound sentiment given that networks of allies are the measure of political and social power in traditional societies.[39] Alone and vulnerable, the Harijan assert the truth of their situation and await religious response. Believers know when Bhairav recognizes the truth of the Harijan claim. He possesses the body of the believer, with hands clawed, teeth barred, and waist bent. He dances on his knees and rolls on the floor. The body of the believer becomes Bhairav's and through this embodiment, the Harijan experience a modicum of healing. The Harijan and cult of Bhairav are important reminders to those of us who call for lament, healing, and justice. Communities of selves-in-relation are called to practice lament for themselves and for others, and in doing so, to manifest the grace of God, to become persons who can recognize subjects who are made other by the doctrines, laws, and structures that would mask injustice.

36. Ibid., 96.
37. Sax, *God of Justice*, 25.
38. Ibid., 32.
39. Ibid., 45.

If we are to become resilient subjects, we must practice public lament—for our identities, for our hopes of what we are to become, the losses of what we will never be, and our complicity in violence and harm. We must presume loss and failure as conditions for recognition, and subsequently the means by which we become resilient people. As we petition the future, potential arcs in the relationships of our lives open and close against a horizon that we cannot predict or know fully. Thus, lament requests an increased consciousness of the relationships that move us in order to inform a pastoral theology and care which refrains from judgment, on the one hand, and on the other hand, resists the cultivation of cultural blinders that disable responses of recognition. Blindness is a universal condition, but, by the conditions it evokes, it is also the very same thing that helps us to see how healing and transformation are made possible.

## To Perform, Participate, and Confront

Our ability to lament and to grieve elicits the conditions for recognition. We seek recognition when we perform and participate in social identities even as they articulate on our lives in ways that we can never fully predict. In performing and participating, we enable the capacity for confrontation and the emotive capacity for righteous anger when we are given accounts of ourselves that misrecognize or which refuse to recognize us or those Others we love. Building from Butler, performances can be acts of hopeful participation and resilience, even when our performance is initially understood to be one in which identity recognition is sought and conferred. In this section, I will draw from several theologians and theorists to more fully describe how our performances of participation and confrontation work to overcome our misrecognition and non-recognition.

In the essay "Unconforming Becomings: The Significance of Whitehead's Novelty and Butler's Subversion for the Repetitions of Lesbian Identity and the Expansion of the Future," Christina K. Hutchins problematizes her participation in a denominational conference meeting of the United Church of Christ.[40] She recounts being anxious and troubled by the structure of the meeting, which was called to address multiculturalism and identity. The planners of the meeting had asked her to participate as "the lesbian representative." She argues that though their intentions came from a place of engaging diversity, they othered gay

40. Hutchins, "Unconforming Becomings," 122–23.

men and lesbians by asking them to speak as if their primary identity was limited to their sexuality. She explains,

> While the planners of the multicultural discussions had some sensitivity to issues of race, sexual orientation, and other "isms," the fact was that there were a designated "gay" and "lesbian" but no "heterosexual" representative. All other participants of various ethnic and social categories were presumed to be heterosexual, an unexamined operation of heteronormativity in which gay men and lesbians were defined as "Other."[41]

Hutchins thoughtfully and graciously turns a potential interpersonal and pastoral conflict into a learning opportunity. When it was her turn to speak, she introduced herself and stated that she "was asked to participate as a lesbian."[42] She offered the persons gathered two gifts that lesbians bring to the church. The first is an attention to the embodied nature of faith. The second is a realization that identities are cultural constructs and fluid in their nature, with the outcome that "the categories themselves and act of categorization, while often helpful, are also restrictive."[43] Her decision to verbalize herself as a participant and not an identity reflects a hope-filled consciousness of doing an identity over being identity. As well, her second gift points to the resilience of subjects in spite of categories that limit. Rather than fixing one identity to her self-in-relation, she instead delineates how others might to choose to participate more fluidly when she speaks from a place of "as." By refusing to introduce herself by stating, "I am a lesbian," she models the work of self-recognition which balances contingency of identity without fixation or stasis.

Doing an identity is a hopeful participation.[44] Participation in an identity acknowledges the fluidity and ad hoc nature of an identity without taking away from the fact that identities can wound us as well as bolster us. Participation is an action which draws us toward hope. In participation we come to see that claims of "I am…" do not define the whole of who we are, that identities need not be fixed, that growth and transformation are possibilities. Further, participation has the ability to give rise to hope, just as hope gives rise to participation. Pastoral theologian Susan Dunlap identities five qualities of hope. She writes that it is an

41. Ibid., 123.

42. Ibid.

43. Ibid.

44. McClure, *Moving Beyond Individualism*, 203–13.

*action*, that it is *specific*, that it *"means patience,"* that it is *rebellious*, and that it is *communal*.[45] Participation in an identity—which is given and chosen, done and undone, a cause and rising of subjectivity—ought not be separated from hope, even in the face of systems and persons which cause our subjection. Rather, participation in an identity ought to reflect these same characteristics—action, specificity, patience, rebellion, and community.

Our hope-filled participation is performed resilience. In the face of setbacks, domination, oppression, and injustice, we perform resilience in the everyday practices of our lives. We pursue the big pictures items of our lives—health, healing, good and paying work, spirituality, loving families of origin and choice—but we also mourn and lament the people that we cannot be in a particular time and place because of structures that would dominate us. Still, we resist and become more resilient. Like exposure to a disease through vaccination, exposure to ideologies whose normal operations cause harm builds up our immunity. Immunity does not mean that the infection cannot invade our bodies and our lives; it can and does. Immunity means that our bodies and our lives are learning how to be unsuitable hosts to diseases that cause personal, social, political, or pastoral subordination and oppression. Becoming an unsuitable host may require performances that confront systems of sin and oppression.

Performances of resilience, like some gender performances, are intended to elicit discomfort. In the face of everyday violence which forms, deforms, informs, reforms, and potentially transforms subjectivity, hope-filled participation must make room for confrontation of systems and persons who would avert their gaze of recognition.[46] Confrontation is a key piece of a performance of resilience. When a subject confronts, she gazes at herself as well as at another subject. Like Butler's mourning, confrontation employs self-reflexivity. However, it can be carried out in various emotional keys, often with layers of dissonant chords: longing and desire, love for self and other, and anger and frustration.

In *Black Skin, White Masks*, psychoanalyst and postcolonial theorist Frantz Fanon shows us the power of confrontation as a performance

45. Dunlap, *Counseling Depressed Women*, 122–25.

46. Scheper-Hughes, *Death Without Weeping*, 272. Scheper-Hughes describes the averted gaze as "the turning away of the state and its agents in their failure to see, to acknowledge what should be right before their eyes." The averted gaze is juxtaposed with Michel Foucault's hostile gaze of the state (1975, 1980) which surveys, punishes, and disciplines the sick and deviant population.

of resilience. He begins by describing the binds of recognition when he petitions the very same dominator who has bound him by his race and gender to recognize him as a black man.

> Locked in this suffocating reification, I appealed to the Other so that his liberating gaze, gliding over my body suddenly smoothed of rough edges, would give me back the lightness of being I thought I had lost, and taking me out of the world put me back in the world. But just as I get to the other slope I stumble, and the Other fixes me with his gaze, his gestures and attitude, the same way you fix a preparation with a dye.[47]

Fanon asks the Other to recognize him as a black man in order to rehumanize him. He is seen and then misrecognized. The Other fixes him in his subject position, making it impossible for him to be anything except black. He is not a man because he is black. He is dehumanized, again.

Yet, Fanon implies that he, like O, participates in his objectification through non-resistance. He writes, "Disoriented, incapable of confronting the Other, the white man, who had no scruples about imprisoning me, I transported myself on that particular day far, very far, from my self, and gave myself up as an object."[48] We would be mistaken to assume that Fanon is an active participant in his own subjection. Instead, the systems of coloniality, race, and gender enlist his desire for recognition. "There were some who wanted to equate me with my ancestors, enslaved and lynched: I decided I would accept this."[49] Like O, his becoming a man in the eyes of others requires his submission. Yet, he cannot become a man in their eyes because he gives the appearance of submission, an act that cannot constitute his subjectivity as male. This is an unconscionable bind.

Unlike O, Fanon has an epiphany. Despite his submission, "the white world, the only decent one, was preventing me from participating."[50] He recognizes the bind of recognition and decides "to make [him]self known" through confrontation.[51] He confronts the systems and those who would dehumanize him through non-recognition and misrecognition even as he seeks recognition. He gives us a short dialogue to demonstrate. A white woman says, "Look how handsome that Negro is." He

47. Fanon, *Black Skin, White Masks*, 89.

48. Ibid., 92.

49. Ibid.

50. Ibid., 94.

51. Ibid., 95.

replies, "The handsome Negro says, 'Fuck you,' madame."[52] He aggressively asserts himself and restores some sense of his own agency. He desires recognition but refuses to allow the Other to misrecognize him. He jams the machinery of iterative injustice by exposing his objectification vis a vis the mechanism of the white gaze. This is the lie that Fanon actively deconstructs in his performance—that "what is called the black soul is a construction by white folk."[53]

Further, Fanon's response is worth considering as a theological performance of liberation. His confrontation instigates the capacity for personal transformation which makes possible social transformation. For it is not only Fanon who is locked in the gaze, but also the gazer who is equally locked by what she cannot see. As such, pastoral theologians and ministers ought not shy away from confrontations or aggressive assertions, whether we are the ones making them or the ones hearing them. As feminist pastoral theologian Kathleen Greider notes, aggression is neither inherently negative or positive, but is part of "human createdness," important to psychospiritual health, and indispensable to justice-making.[54] The ability to be effective change-agents and caregivers requires an embodied capacity to listen for testimonies of resilience and to support resistance to harmful personal and social relationships and the effects of structural violence. To do otherwise is to fail to recognize the injustices that impede the growth of our imaginations, our hearts, and our embodied selves-in-relation.

In this chapter I took up descriptions of how structural violence and political repression affect subject formation. I argued that cultivating the capability to lament and to confront are critical junctures for subjects and social groups who experience misrecognition and non-recognition. Like care and justice, lamentation and confrontation are two sides of the same coin. Seeing both, as well as seeing where both might be but are absent, is critical for the ongoing task of recognition for feminist pastoral theologians. In the next chapter, I describe a feminist pastoral theology of recognition and a praxis of encounter in order to more adequately inform feminist pastoral theological anthropology.

52. Ibid., 94.

53. Ibid., xviii.

54. Greider, "'Too Militant'? Aggression, Gender, and the Construction of Justice," 124.

# 7

## *Encountering Other Subjects*

Those who suffer from structural violence, political repression, domination, and interpersonal and familial injustice ought to be afforded recognition. Yet they are not, and this is precisely the problem. Despite the desire to recognize and affirm persons, we all are subject to conscious and unconscious blindness. Appeals to identity are one way to ensure recognition. The accounts that are heard, as well as those that are misheard or not heard, bear testimony to the fact that economic misdistribution is not the sole cause of injustice and oppression, but in fact is deeply tied to the perception of one's identity. Caring about injustice and caring about identity is critical in order to advance a pastoral praxis which enables persons to become self-determining, flourishing selves-in-relation. It is for this central reason that I have dialogued with theories of recognition in order to inform a feminist pastoral theology of recognition attentive to subject formation.

We cannot rid ourselves of identity. It would be folly for those who suffer injustice in relationship to their chosen and given identities. It would be hubris on the part of those whose chosen and given identities uphold destructive ideologies. The failures of recognition urge us to identify ways to recognize other subjects, including internalized Others, in ways that are not in the modalities of domination, submission, or repression. In this chapter I describe a praxis of encounter grounded in the discipline of feminist pastoral theology. We have the opportunity to be transformed when we encounter others subjects, including those internal subjects whom we have cast out. We reflect on the ghosts of our own subjugation so that we may become hope and joy-filled agents of transformation.

## A Feminist Pastoral Theology of Recognition

Here, I return to the discipline of feminist pastoral theology to outline themes of recognition. In outlining these themes, I hope to show how recognition informed praxis impacts how the discipline critically gives and receives accounts of the self-in-relation. Throughout this text I argued that we must pay attention to identity, particularly to the personal and social identities by which selves-in-relation experience physical, emotional, and social paucity and violence. At the same time, I urged us to be careful (and full of care) so that we do not mistake attending to identity as the real work that must be done as co-participants in the joyful becoming of the kin-dom of God. I offer these summative points as a starting place toward a feminist pastoral theology of recognition and a praxis of encounter.

*First, a feminist pastoral theology of recognition attends to the making of selves-in-relation at the porous and historical peripheries of the intrapsychic, interpersonal, social-political, and theological.* The interplay between intrapersonal, interpersonal, social, and theological relations are dynamically co-constructive of subjectivity. Further, each element is both historically situated, materially embodied, and influential in creating the internal and external psychosocial environment of subjects. Persons who are denigrated at a social and theological level absorb that denigration intrapsychically and may engage in interpersonal relationships where that denigration is played out again, often between persons of opposite gender. These are conditions by which oppression and subjugation are made possible. With other feminist pastoral theologians who have contributed to linking the interpersonal and social realms, a feminist pastoral theology of recognition attends to the spiraling levels of complexity while making connections between the individual, larger socio-political issues of injustice, and theological claims which may uphold or tear down oppression.

*Second, a feminist pastoral theology of recognition is critically aware of how human needs and capabilities are enlisted to oppress and subjugate*

*persons, as well as how they might be taken up to liberate selves-in-relation.*
With Jessica Benjamin we learned that persons are capable of recognition
and assertion. Because the circuits of recognition and assertion are both
capabilities and needs, the desire for recognition can morph from circuits
to shackles. Reading *The Story of O*, we saw that withheld recognition
creates a psychic need which is filled by submission to an external source
of authority. In reading Nella Larsen's *Passing* with Judith Butler we saw
that Clare's need for recognition is fulfilled through her misrecognition
and subsequent passing as a white woman. Rather than ask for an external authority to confer recognition and interpret her performance as
"correct" or "incorrect," Clare games the system that would expose her
body as black, and thus an incorrect performance, and passes as white.
With Marcella Althaus-Reid, we saw that even theologies which have the
intention to build selves- and communities-in-relation may be co-opted
by ideologies which enslave not only selves and communities, but God's
very self. A pastoral theology of recognition looks toward all these dimensions in order to articulate how a subject is constituted by needs and
capabilities, but also possesses the ability to subvert systems.

*Third, a feminist pastoral theology of recognition identifies critical
interventions, practices, and programs that are attentive to the affective
dimensions of life as they are expressed in relationships, verbally, and
through the body.* We are called to rewire the shackles of domination and
submission so that they become circuits of recognition and assertion.
Rewiring requires that both genders participate in the work of recognition and assertion by balancing the tension. For pastoral theologians, this
work occurs at interpersonal and social levels, grounded in a theological
worldview of God as love. As pastoral theologians have long noted, the
practices of one-on-one pastoral care and pastoral counseling provide
opportunities to recognize persons who seek confirmation of their assertion of selfhood. At the social level, when communities of care and
persons of faith stand in solidarity with those who are dominated, they
assert the need for recognition, especially when structural violence and
political repression would have us mistake silence or indifference for
consent. In these tasks, the "negative" affective dimensions of life, such
as lamentation and aggressive assertion, are indicators of injustice and
ought to be cultivated by caregivers who seek to end oppression and
domination.

At the same time, lament and aggression are not only verbal activities. Like submission and oppression, they are also visible on the body of

the subject. Grinding poverty and structural violence leave their traces on stooped bodies, ill bodies, and emotionless bodies that are gendered and raced, often feminized, colonized, or colored. Bodies speak when words fail. Thus, a feminist pastoral theology of subjectivity is attentive to the physical, material body as a means of communicating the need and capacity for both recognition and assertion when emotions are incapacitated.

*Fourth, a feminist pastoral theology of recognition is attentive to the particularities of difference in the constellation of gender, sexuality, ability, and race/ethnicity, but not constrained by the categories of identity.* Histories of abuse and oppression must be told through the lens of identity. In doing so, we actively give and receive accounts of the self-in-relation which enable collective action. Collective and coalitional action in support of identities which we may or may not individually share begets necessary social change. Even though we may not know fully the effects of social change, as theologians we hope that these changes lead to transformation of stony hearts to hearts of flesh.

Still, at wholly other times, our identities do us in ways beyond our control. With Judith Butler we learned that we cannot trust that being a certain gender affords us recognition. One's gender is made and remade through a series of repeated norms—norms which call us to account for ourselves and which give us a mandate to do gender correctly. Those who do not do their gender correctly, or any of the other identities we inhabit, may be condemned for their failure. A feminist pastoral theology of recognition is keenly aware that identity cannot be forgotten in analysis, but also navigates with intention and skill through uses of identity that would fix or make stable a subject's position. Thus, for those who undergo a transformation through the practice of recognition, heart speaks to heart, *cor ad cor*, so that one is both one's identities and also more than any identity category might ever capture.

*Fifth, a feminist pastoral theology of recognition reflects on and enables just caring practices through the cultivation of self-reflexivity as we encounter an Other, including an internalized Other.* Rethinking gender as an unstable category gives us pause as pastoral theologians. While it opens wide a veranda of possibility, the instability of gender also asks us to develop a practice of just care to attend to subjects who have been elided by misrecognition, unintelligibility, or non-recognition. While feminist pastoral theologians cannot ensure that every subject or social group is recognized, as this is an impossible task, we can practice and teach a certain self-reflexivity that is based on participation in systems which are imperfect and unjust but which we change through assertion of resilient agency in the face of harmful structures, as we come to understand what these things are. But, we must be willing to see, both internally and externally who is othered.

We veer away from well-mapped out routes in order to encounter subjects who are not us. A self-reflexive practice of relational encounter hopes that we learn about their own, and our own, becoming. When major newspapers and other media sources of information refuse to speak about some kinds of lives, like the murdered Palestinian family, we seek out sources who will speak to us about the frailty and the resiliency of subjects caught in the webs of interpersonal, religious, social, and political relationships so that we may know more about the human condition and think toward interpersonal, infrastructural, and superstructural change. When we seek out sources unlike ourselves (which also may be in ourselves) we enable our capability to mourn the things that we are not and will never be. We enact a theo-praxis which beckons us to confront the sources of our self-making. We approach this kind of endeavor with a spirit of humility in order to resist participation in a reification process that vilifies, condemns, or others subjects. Instead, we invite the Other, and are invited by the Other, to listen carefully. We acknowledge that at times we may not be able to listen or cannot hear. We acknowledge the limitations and the incommensurability of knowing in this relational way of being. This too—the frustration of not being able to connect, the frustration of not being understood, the frustration of never fully knowing or understanding the totality of a self-in-relation—spurs moments of self-reflexivity.

*Sixth, doing just care requires analysis of that which is repudiated in theologies of identity, particularly in relationship to sex/gender/desire.* Marcella Althaus-Reid candidly notes that the illusion-building structures of liberation theology and its inattention to its own heteronormativity reveals that even emancipatory aiming theological discourse can miss the mark. Additionally, in Butler, individual identities map social power, and are constituted through each other and through the repudiation of the external and internal other. So, for example, the "most" "straight" "man" can only be straight by his vehement denial of a feminized homosexuality. He must close that door—and foreclose any future relationships that seem to take on homosexual qualities—in order to be straight. His denial of a possible homosexual future makes the present irrevocably straight. His disavowal and repudiation of a potential self-identity is thus projected outward. He must disdain, hate, or even loathe that which he fears could be part of himself. Theology can proceed in the very same way. Theologies are constructed and disseminated which either elide or bless the blindness, including a liberation theology which retains heteropatriarchy as a normative framework. All who seek to liberate, but especially pastoral theologians, are called to show the linkages between the disavowed and feared other, and the subject's formation through unexamined, but deeply held, theological ideology. Moreover, pastoral theologians play a central role in creating and disseminating new theological visions in response to harmful ideologies.

*Seventh, a feminist pastoral theology of recognition, while serious, encourages imagination and play in order to resist a limiting or fixed identity discourse.* For persons who are already conscious of their own interpersonal or socio-political oppression and subjugation through ethnicity/race, gender/sex, theological, colonial and capitalist forces, playful but serious tactics of resistance give rise to alternative, sometimes intentional, visions of living as a subject of interpersonal, social, and theological hegemonies and as an agent within those very constraints.[1] While acknowledging the depths of pain, suffering, and death, we playfully and joyfully instigate opportunities for personal and social transformation, not knowing fully what we are petitioning and how we will be changed, but trusting that resiliency, self- and communal-determination, and freedom make a beautiful way.

## Intentional Listening through Social Geography

Feminist pastoral theologians are charged to care for selves-in-relation and communities which are often organized by identity and affiliation. We are charged to care for marginalized and oppressed persons who suffer. As we seek out those selves-in-relation, we reflect on the lived experience of subjects. In the preceding chapters I have called us to reflect on the problem and solution of recognition as a critical component of subject formation. In doing so, we ascertain what contributions theories of recognition make to theorizing in feminist pastoral theology as well

1. Certeau, *The Practice of Everyday Life*, 34. Certeau invokes tactics as one modality to effect change which holds in tension cultural symbolic systems and the actions of participants in these systems (xi).

as what contributions feminist pastoral theology make toward the development of theories of recognition. Allow me to restate the problem of recognition one more time in order to develop a grounded, spatially-oriented feminist pastoral theology.

The problem of recognition is precisely that there are selves-in-relation who are misrecognized or not recognized at all. Recognizing othered selves-in-relations of care requires psyche driven acts of assertion that manifest in voiced or embodied claims for care and justice. When subjects are habituated into their own submission or oppression, their voiced or embodied claims of assertion are misinterpreted as consent or indifference. This is misrecognition and requires thoughtful mechanisms to correctly hear accounts that insist on interpersonal, social, and theological recognition, that is, when the subjects desire to be heard. We must keep in mind that passing, although a misrecognition, is a powerful tool given the contraints of social systems and individuals within those systems which harm.

In addition to subjects who are misrecognized, there are subjects who are not recognized at all. In interpersonal relationships with persons unlike themselves, these subjects may also experience non-recognition of the specific conditions of difference that affect their experience of suffering. Non-recognition of subjects and groups of difference at the social-political level indicates the state of political-moral discourse within a given society. That is, social recognition is conferred by a public that supports organized social groups who articulate and assert their claims of inequity. While the task of building a social movement is crucial for large scale conscientization, it does not ensure recognition of persons and groups who suffer injustices that have not reached the level of mass perception. Social theorist Axel Honneth reflects on this problem, writing,

> Only experiences of suffering that have crossed the threshold of mass media attention are confirmed as morally relevant, and we are unable to advocatorially thematize and make claims about socially unjust states of affairs that have so far been deprived of public attention . . . It is all too easy to abstract from social suffering and injustice that, owing to the filtering effects of the bourgeois public sphere, has not yet reached the level of political thematization and organization.[2]

---

2. Fraser and Honneth, *Redistribution or Recognition?*, 115.

Non-recognition means that a subject's claims for care and justice have not yet been heard by those with authority to recognize; it does not follow the subject is failing to assert herself.

Reaching a level of political thematization and organization requires pastoral interventions that demonstrate how psychosocial harms of misrecognition and non-recognition are perpetuated through structural violence, political repression, and ideological machinations. Recognizing other subjects as a pastoral intervention requires a grounded ministry of critical presence. Recognizing other subjects in the context of theology in practice invites conversation with diverse fields that assist us to critically see. Social geography is one such partner for pastoral theology. Social geography provides a critical reflection process in which we may begin to see recognition and subjectivity as *located* theological processes, not only intersubjective or social processes. Its methods link social phenomena and spatiality by bringing social theory into dialogue with physical sites, cartography, and geography. Additionally, a conversation between social geography and pastoral theology can be mutually beneficial when we consider the situatedness of religious and theological practice. For example, what are the situated intersubjective, social, and physical locations which make the cult of Bhairav a theologically significant tactic of lament, aggression, and resistance? Could the cult of Bhairav have such influence on another group of low-caste people in a different region or in a different terrain?

Social geography is closely linked to the major sub-discipline of human geography in the discipline of geography. While human geography maps people, communities, and cultures in relationship to human activities (health, politics, population, economy, development), social geography appropriates qualitative research methodologies to site and critique structural inequities. For example, well-known social geographer Manuel Castells uses a Marxist framework to show that "cities, as we see and experience them, inscribe in concrete the history of contested power, successes, failures, and compromises within capitalism."[3] Radical cartographers perform social geographies by physically mapping political, social, and personal realities that, echoing Butler, we are asked not to see, including subjects who are misrecognized or not recognized at all.[4] Two themes of social geography are valuable tools for analysis to feminist

---

3. Susser, *The Castells Reader*, 3.
4. See *An Atlas of Radical Cartography* (Mogel and Bhagat) for examples.

pastoral theology as we grapple with the complex realities of personal and social suffering and their effects on a subject's being and becoming. First, social geography expands care of the living human web to encompass ill- or mis-charted locations of the marginalized and oppressed subjects who we are asked not to see. Second, social geography reads the living texts of persons and bodies on the street and in the neighborhood to legitimate and illuminate local knowledge, including lived knowledge on the harms that come to subjugated selves-in-relation.

Social geography navigates the relationship between social space and physical space. As a corollary, intrapsychic and interpsychic space may also be charted by accounting for the relationship between subject formation as an iterative socially constructive and localized process. However, it is critical to remember that though iterative, subject formation through social construction is not reducible to a predetermined result that would constrict agency. Instead the space of subject formation is the place where agency is made possible and exercised in innovative and unpredictable ways. If one aspect of intersubjective recognition gone awry masks the assertions of persons and populations, and if pastoral caregivers are to stand in solidarity embodying lamentation and confrontation to structural violence (and as a means to mirror personal capacities for self- and communal-determination rather than submission), then tools are needed to increase visibility of persons in social-spatial settings. Said another way, practicing recognition of the self-in-relation is also spatially determined. As such, spatial interventions are critical loci for practices of pastoral care that attend to those who have yet to press claims for recognition in socially acceptable ways as well as for those whose intersectionality results in unmitigated misrecognition or non-recognition.

Spatiality as a lens to view intrapsychic, intersubjective, and social suffering reinforces and expands a central concept in feminist pastoral theology: that the living human web is also a physically situated web. This concept is also reinforced in the multi-authored text *Weight of the World*, where sociologist Pierre Bourdieu elaborates the relationship between the personal, social, and spatial. He writes, "Because social space is inscribed at once in spatial structures and in the mental structures that are partly produced by the incorporation of these structures, space is one of the sites where power is asserted and exercised, and no doubt, in its subtlest form, as symbolic violence that goes unperceived as violence."[5]

5. Bourdieu, "Site Effects," 126.

The effects of spatial neglect mark a region, and the people who live in it, as *verboten*: tough neighborhoods, dangerous neighborhoods, spaces filled with others who are expelled from social-political discourse, those who are seen as not fully being human selves-in-relation, those denied parity of participation.

As a field of study and a research practice, social geography questions the marking out of the *verboten* regions through situated social analysis. Further, it has the possibility of dismantling the moralistic geography that judges before intellectual analysis, affective engagement, or theological perception. Situated as a response to the devastating effect of Hurricane Katrina, geographer James C. Fraser uses the phrase *moral geography* to critique how FEMA officials framed relocation from the 100-year floodplains as a responsibility to mitigate the risks for self and others. Fraser argues that such an argument is "individualistic and focuses on rationalizing people's decision making to create a moral geography of sorts that legitimates the dismantling of state protection for social welfare."[6] Fraser's claim points to Bourdieu's insight that spatiality, socio-political identities and locations, and intersubjectivity shape subjects and affect their self-determinative capabilities for flourishing. Instead of referring to victims of Hurricane Katrina as poor people who *chose* to live in flood plains, Fraser's insight points us toward seeing the limitation of any such choosing, especially when overlaid with a moralistic code by which society can split those subjects from itself and thus absolve itself of the responsibility to care for all selves-in-relation.

While large scale disasters bring our attention to social suffering and structural violence in dramatic ways, spatial analysis urges us to consider how the "silent riots of everyday life" are habituated and inhabited through claims made by space on agents, and agents on that very same space.[7] One result of social geography in pastoral theological practice encourages the reading of the living texts of persons and bodies on the street and in the neighborhood, not just those in the hospital room, the church nave, the caregiver's office, or the counselor's private room. Reading the situated living human web legitimates and illuminates local knowledge, and may serve as a prophetic witness to the transforming power of resistance. Though not a far cry from the practice of visiting the faithful as pastoral care or peripatetic spiritual practices such as pilgrimage, I am

---

6. Fraser, "The Relevance of Human Geography for Studying Urban Disasters," 16.

7. Wacquant, "America as Social Dystopia," 133.

suggesting that social geography for pastoral practice encourages *contact* with the "non-faithful," with the outcast, with the sinner, leper, and tax-collector, with the Other whose recognition hinges upon my willingness to be in relation, and upon whom my recognition hinges.

Contact as pastoral practice contains internal goods that enable feminist pastoral theologians to give more adequate accounts of the self-in-relation. In order to adequately cultivate the theo-social practices of lament, resiliency, and confrontation that enable a pastoral theology of recognition, as well as the practice of encounter that I develop in what follows, we must understand them as actions in situated spaces that invoke an imperfect openness toward the other. When pastoral theology enlists social geography, care of the living human web includes explicit attention to the spaces inhabited by selves-in-relation. Ill- or mis-charted locations of the marginalized and oppressed subjects who we are asked not to see begin to make claims upon our lives, and we may choose a daring care response.

## A Praxis of Encounter

Feminist pastoral theology ought to make stakes with those whose suffering is filtered through interests that would absorb and obscure the commonplace atrocity of suffering. Following an incarnational theology that pays attention to social geography, we pitch our tents with those who are marginalized in society, accompanying each other in a world where brokenness abounds but where grace also lives. In this way, a feminist pastoral theology of recognition also contains a theological praxis of encounter.

As I have argued, the problem of recognition is also the solution: recognition. When those who care offer solace or comfort to persons who hurt, we are afforded the opportunity to pay attention to voiced and embodied claims for recognition. Likewise, communities of faith are called to become places where recognition might become spatially located by opening wide the doors in order to move from pew to street. Just as the filtering effects of the social-political sphere make it so that claims for recognition go unheard in media, a disheartening corollary also exists in the church. Claims of recognition are misheard, underheard, and unheard. Additionally, some claims for recognition are not only mis-, under- or unheard, but heard and made other through vilification masked as orthodoxy or orthopraxis. As such, a praxis of care must also think toward how other selves-in-relation encounter each other.

Countering blindness and vilification is work for the long-haul and requires communal spaces where resilience and hope may come to dwell. In the essay "Resistance Is Not Futile" Church of God in Christ minister and psychotherapist Cedric C. Johnson argues for a heterotopic praxis to enable "the identification and creation of communal spaces of alternate ordering outside of social control." [8] A heterotopic space is central to caring for those who are dispossessed, subaltern, or oppressed. Heterotopic spaces of resistance assist misrecognized and non-recognized subjects to build assertive movements. Heterotopic spaces are the place where we gather to recognize truths within ourselves and with each other about the particularities of suffering due to injustices, whether interpersonal, structural, or political. In heterotopic spaces of resistances, assertive movements can be addressed through empathic care, collective power, political will, and theo-social imaginings. Heterotopic spaces of resistance may be militantly antiracist, antisexist, anticolonial, anticapitalist, and antidogmatic, and thus inherently political, but they are also liminal spaces where care and theology are worked out, sometimes antagonistically, sometimes in more relational ways.

While Johnson uses the verb *create* to signify ways that heterotopic spaces come into existence, I hesitate to use this word because it is possible to co-opt creation for neocolonial strategies of domination, rather than theological in-breakings. I would suggest that theologians and ministers may cultivate, beckon, and realize heterotopic spaces, but ought to resist the urge to create a heterotopic space for o/Others. Heterotopic space resists creation by persons in authority, whether authority is conferred by dominant culture status or religious bodies. As such, creation of a heterotopic space may, in fact, reify homogenizing projects of domination and submission through mechanisms of colonization, occupation, and infiltration. Heterotopic space becomes possible from a praxis of encounter that bears witness to the difficulty and possibility of recognition.

Encountering an othered subject, whether internal or external, is fraught with the possibilities of both conflict and mutuality. Taken from Latin *in + contra*, encounters are meetings in which our face-to-face contact may pit us against another, whether internal or external. Yet, encounters are also unexpected or chance happenings. With the right kind

8. Cedric C. Johnson, "Resistance is Not Futile," 167.

of dispositions—generosity, humility, curiosity, prudence—encounters can also be fruitful. These fruitful encounters are built on recognizing the internal goods of interclass, interethnic, interreligious, intergender/sex contact, and other points of difference.

Samuel R. Delany, Professor of English and Creative Writing at Temple University, describes the goods of contact in *Times Square Red, Times Square Blue*. Written as a performative social-spatial walk-about, Delany invites us to encounter other selves-in-relation. As a long-time visitor to the peep shows, porn theaters, bars, shish kebab vendors, and electronic stores along Forty-second Street in New York City before its Disneyfication, Delany provides us with both photographic images and his personal account of selves-in-relation as we stroll along with him, together reading the street. With him we meet Darrell Deckard, a hustler and "a *good*-looking black man of twenty-six."[9] We learn that Darrell has been hustling for two years and that today's concern is "the Public Morals Squad," e.g. the police, who, according to street wisdom, are hiding in theaters to make arrests.[10] Neither sentimental about the vices of Forty-second Street—drugs, violence, prostitution, sexual public health risks and HIV/AIDS specifically—nor condemning of his subjects, including himself as subject, Delany walks a fine line to bring to our attention to those whom the machinations of recognition would confer a yes, no, or maybe. His method invokes an epistemology that favors movement into and through the subjectivity of those whose lives are foreclosed or denigrated in social space.

Delany counters the detrimental effects of misrecognition or non-recognition by claiming interclass contact and communication in a timbre of good will as virtues. He writes, "Life is at its most rewarding, productive, and pleasant when large numbers of people understand, appreciate, and seek out interclass contact and communication conducted in a mode of good will."[11] As an ode, of sorts, to Times Square, Delany describes how redevelopment displaced contact as a social practice and lifts up what was made possible through interclass contact.

Prior to its Disneyification, Times Square was a place where interclass contact was possible among gay men seeking sex. Peep shows, sex shops, bars, and movie theaters were the physical spaces where

9. Delany, *Times Square Red, Times Square Blue*, 10.

10. Ibid., 11.

11. Ibid., 111.

sexual contact between two men of different classes could occur over and against the social practices that would encourage class warfare between them. According to Delany the happenstance nature of contact—similar pleasurable pursuits conducted within a geographic area—produces unexpected goods. He gives the example of connecting a recent ex-Jesuit priest to a job opportunity in publishing as well as a chance encounter with a man who became a long-term partner. His point is that interclass contact encourages "important or dramatic" occurrences as strangers with various social goods and social needs interact with each other in public space.[12] Public spaces which encourage homogeneity and remove "dangerous" elements—homosexuals, anarchists, persons of color, religious minorities—disable encounters which may become socially, intersubjectively, or theologically transformative.

While the interclass contact that Delaney describes makes life pleasurable and rewarding, dramatic encounters may also make claims upon those of engaged in caring with othered subjects. When pastoral theologians and religious leaders dare to risk a caring response, we must be willing to acknowledge the limitations of our knowing even as we commit ourselves to encounter, accompany, and stand in solidarity with othered subjects. I would like to suggest that tactics of encounter are critical pastoral skills for caring about justice. Those who engage in encounter employ tactics to out-maneuver the structural systems that do violence by rendering Other all persons who do not live up to the normative ideal. Following social theorist Michel de Certeau, a feminist pastoral praxis of encounter is built on the uncertainty of possessing a space, and thus relies on mobility. Encounters are tactical in nature, and therefore are full of uncertainty and mobility. Certeau writes that a tactic is "a calculated action determined by the absence of a proper locus."[13] A tactic is a play made by those who do not hold strategic powers. Tactical encounters are not premeditated or planned. In addition to those who work through programs and policies toward the psychological and social recognition of vulnerable populations whose suffering is intelligible, practitioners of encounter "seize on the wing the possibilities that offer themselves at any given moment."[14] Tactics of encounter are timely, and thus resist being overtaken by systems, institutions, or persons who exercise power. In

12. Ibid., 169.

13. Certeau, *The Practice of Everyday Life*, 37.

14. Ibid.

tactics, time cannot be possessed, only passed. Thus, timing becomes a critical intervention in asserting and recognizing. We resist homogeneity and fixity, embrace uncertainty and mobility, and encounter other and othered selves-in-relation again and again as the horizons of time and space stretch forward and also foreclose.

How might a praxis of tactical encounter be embodied and culti-vated in ministry and theological education? Let me suggest one image for ministry that pushes beyond the traditional boundaries of pastor, pastoral care specialist, or faith-based activist, and which responds to the interpersonal and social need to assert and to recognize as well as the constraint of achieving these ends. The image I have in mind is the street journalist. This image trades on the cultivation of skills and practical know-how that epitomize the feminist pastoral theological endeavor—listening, empathy, mutuality, justice, care, attention to difference—and put these skill sets to use through images that encourage their deploy-ment in extra-pastoral temporal and spatial locations. If it is true that claims for recognition are silenced and obscured, not that there is a fail-ure of assertion, then it follows that one response to this dilemma is the cultivation of persons who are capable of hearing assertions even when social practices and institutions would silence or obscure those claims. The street journalist is a person who can do so as a roving listener and a social critic.

As roving listeners, street journalists form relationships with situ-ated individuals. A roving, listening street journalist engages in heart-to-heart conversations to strengthen relationships between persons and institutions.[15] They appreciate the assets, or gifts, of selves-in-relation in order to build opportunities for transformation and growth, which includes identifying personal, social, political, and theological oppor-tunities. A roving, listening street journalist encounters subjects in the hopes of building relationships where dreams and hopes can be shared. They listen closely to the stories of frustration, anger, mourning, and la-ment, as well as the stories and half-told stories of oppression that are stated without emotion. A roving, listening street journalist is peripatetic, walking along the paved streets and sidewalks as well as carving through the unsanctioned routes that those who do not hold power use to move

15. King, "Death and Resurrections of an Urban Church," para. 11. I was first introduced to this idea by leading reflective practitioners Susan Rans and Mary H. Nelson at a faculty seminar on asset-based community development at the Institute of Pastoral Studies, Loyola University Chicago.

through territory. They engage subjectivity through their roving and listening. They encounter other subjects at a grassroots level that promotes inter-difference contact.

Street journalists are also social critics. They actively engage in analysis and criticism of "values, practices, and norms" in their daily life that silence voices or make voices go unheard and unrecognized.[16] Street journalists as social critics gather knowledge about those silenced voices. Though they attempt to make social change, the work of the street journalist is not guaranteed success. Political theorist Brooke Ackerly explains that "social criticism is one way to counter, mitigate, or undermine power inequalities, but whether a particular effort will be effective is a matter of politics."[17] As such, street journalists as social critics "promote inquiry, opportunities for deliberation, and institutional changes that facilitate broadly informed and inclusive deliberations."[18] They are self-reflexive, and potentially multi-sited, moving between communities to develop critical edges necessary to call attention to inequalities in social decision-making.[19]

The street journalist deftly maneuvers amongst persons, neighborhoods, and institutions to hear and recognize the complexity of selves-in-relation living under constraints which they may or may not have the ability to choose freely, but which nonetheless are, in part, determinative of their becoming. Street journalists tell these stories in their complexity, moving between personal experiences of misrecognition or non-recognition to indictment of social-political systems, and from message to action. The venue and mode of analysis and action is largely dependent upon the skill set and artistic vision of the street journalist. She may be a printmaker, a writer, a filmmaker, a musician, a theologian-minister, a radical. A street journalist is a way of life more than a profession; she pursues leads that come from the people and frames them as claims of injustice that must be rectified through personal and social transformation as well as mutual love and care.

One example is that of hip-hop duo Rebel Diaz, brothers Rodrigo Venegas (Rodstarz) and Gonzalo Venegas (G1). Based in the South Bronx, they actively work to call attention to systemic injustices. As *periodistas*

16. Ackerly, *Political Theory and Feminist Social Criticism*, 13.

17. Ibid., 5.

18. Ibid., 150.

19. Ibid., 155.

*de la esquina*, or street journalists, they make normative assertions for recognition with and as subjects who suffer injustices from the everyday violence of capitalism, racism, and xenophobia, as well as the social violences which make themselves visible in police brutality, deportations, and the incarceration of persons of color.[20] Their music speaks to social movements of resistance and liberation, like the execution of prisoner Troy Davis and the Occupy Wall Street movement. While the sound itself is unique, the lyrics of the bilingual duo offer social critique. In the song "Guilty" they perform a lyrical trial of systems and institutions that do harm to persons of color, convicting the prison industrial complex, "the capitalist system of America, the U.S. military, the FBI, CIA, ATF, ICE, Homeland Security, and the neighborhood police."[21] These performed lyrics are bold assertions in response to oppressive systems and persons who are complicit in misrecognition and non-recognition. They posit their assertions as convictions of multiple oppressors and systems of oppression.

In another song, they sample the civil rights freedom song, "Which Side Are You On?" and use this question to outline an extensive list of whose side they are on based on claims for human rights. They answer, "I'm on the side of the workers, the teachers and lunch ladies, on the streets with brown mommies raisin' our brown babies. I'm with youth organizers cleaning up the Bronx River. I'm with Jaime Escalante when I stand and deliver."[22] As street journalists, they listen and critique, but they also act for transformations of selves-in-relation. Settling in the Mott Haven area of the South Bronx, the duo and their former partner, Lah Tere, established the Rebel Diaz Arts Collective (RDACBX). Using a former warehouse, the RDACBX builds community through the arts, especially hip-hop and multi-media. They teach youth how to use hip-hop as a tool for social commentary, developing programs and curriculum for critical thinking and political education.[23]

As street journalists, Rebel Diaz performs a praxis of encounter that is based in the knowledge that encounters are not always pleasant and that systems of power resist hearing accounts of oppressed selves-in-relation. This is modeled in their lyrics as well as in their everyday lives.

---

20. Rebel Diaz, "Que'Sta Pasando! (Featuring Divine of the D.E.Y.)."
21. Rebel Diaz, "Guilty."
22. Rebel Diaz, "Which Side Are You On?"
23. Beekman, "Hip-hop won't stop in the South Bronx," para. 4.

On June 18, 2008, Rodstarz and G1 witnessed a street vendor selling fruit being harassed by New York City police. They went over toward the vendor and the police. According to witnesses, when the brothers asked the police officers for their badge numbers, the police officers became agitated, beat them with billy clubs, and charged them resisting arrest and assault.[24] This face-to-face meeting was an encounter of conflict. At the same time, this encounter had ripple effects beyond the control of the police officers or the brothers. After their arrest 150 people gathered outside the precinct to demand their release, and a year after their arrest the charges were dropped by Judge Darcel Clark who cited their impressive community involvement and urged them to "keep up the good work."[25]

I have described the elements of encounter and the image of the street journalist but have yet to speak as to why encounter is needed for a theological praxis of recognition. Acts of recognition and assertion require an engagement. To witness is only a first step when we seek to know something about the subject whose suffering is mutually reinforced by psychological, social, theological, and spatial forces. To witness is not enough when so many forces inside of ourselves and external to ourselves keep us from recognizing subjects who stand with us, and even within us. And yet, our finitude and the nature of the future keep us from ever fully plumbing the depths of another. In fact, without that distance recognition and assertion are not possible.

It is the impossible but hopeful task of recognizing other subjects that our pastoral feminist praxis asks of us. When we encounter other subjects we are offered opportunities to learn to love differently. We learn to love in a way that acknowledges our human frailty and conditions of social sin that we did not choose, but continue to live through. Though love beckons us to recognize, to care, to attend to the othered parts of ourselves and of subjects outside ourselves in intersubjective recognition, we also know that our capacity to do so fails. It would be easy to harbor disillusion deep in our beings while living between suffering and flourishing.

Disillusion and disenchantment cannot be undone by maintaining the stories that run as an undercurrent through the Euro-American Christian mythos: hard work brings equal opportunity; dutiful prayer invites divine abundance; emotions are weak; diversity, so long as it does

24. Davey and Jenny, "NYC Police Beat Up Rap Group Members Rebel Diaz," para. 3–4.

25. Noor, "Judge dismisses case against Rebel Diaz," 3.

not challenge the status quo, is a celebration of God's love for all people. We need new stories from the people themselves that incite metanoia, revolution, laughter, tears. New stories (and very old ones) provide metaphors and images for caring, justice, and love that are not beholden to the stasis that impairs recognition. Theologian Laurel Schneider writes, "Once upon a time, poets told stories and theologians explained the stories. Once upon a time, theologians explained their own dreams and visions, and poets gave them wings . . . It is therefore past time for theologians, storytellers, and poets to listen again to each other and inspire one another."[26] Those who care have the opportunity to tell the stories of people, and the stories of God, again.

26. Schneider, *Beyond Monotheism*, 111.

# 8

## *Recognizing the Self-in-Relation*

*"Love flowers best in openness and freedom."*[1]

Earlier this year, Tibetan Buddhist monks from Drepung Gomang Monastery came to my campus to create a sand mandala and to share facets of their culture with students, faculty, staff, and the larger community. The religious practice of making a mandala is painstaking work, accomplished as sand is added grain by grain to a larger whole. It is also an embodied act of love. A mandala is a work in process, revealing itself to be what it is becoming as each grain is tapped into place, with great care, attention, and compassion. When the mandala is completed, it is then destroyed. I went to see it destroyed.

Over one hundred people filled the Gallery San Giuseppe, taking one last look, savoring the richness of color, perhaps taking in the deeper meaning behind the mandala of the Lord of Compassion. I sat on a hard wood bench, also gazing at the mandala. The monks and the people gathered, and the question and answer session began. I did not voice aloud the question I held deep in my heart, which is rooted in my questions of subjectivity: What do we do when we know we must destroy the illusions we hold about the object of our desire in order to recognize subjectivity,

1. Abbey, *Desert Solitaire*, 29.

165

and yet we feel sorrow or anger at its destruction? What do we do when we come to see that the illusions we have passively accepted or actively built around a person or a community of people are not true? Without words, the monks answer my question: we sweep, destroying what we have built in order that the prayers and hopes we have placed with each sand of grain may become blessing to all sentient creatures.

The colored sand grains become mixed and are transmuted, and we release the harsh gritty beauty, now transformed, back into the world. We go to the wide Ohio River. We walk onto a ferry and push away from the shore, from the ground that holds us. We are groundless, floating. We are displaced. We stand with the monks who cast the grains of sand into the churning sediment and liquid of life, curling black and blue. We pray for the awakening of all sentient creatures. The monks lead us in ancient practices that reveal what they make us as we become. I laugh and cry at the same time like a mad woman, no, like a wild woman, a hysterical high-pitched throaty sound that convulses my whole body in the car and carries me back to campus. I return to my office at 3 pm on a good Friday, falling to my knees between my desk and my books, my holy shrine to Wisdom, laugh-crying, scribbling notes in my journal to help me hold onto what I now understand theologically about subjectivity through a religious practice.

The paradox of laughing and crying at the same time is not lost on me as I reflect on clinging to the object of desire and the practice of releasing the object I have constructed, even fetishized in my mind, as the ultimate expression of beauty. I want to hold tightly to the object. The wisdom of this religious practice tells me to let it go in order for it to become fully what it already is. I release in order for it to reveal its truest and deepest beauty to me. I release because I recognize.

What is true of the mandala is true of our treatment of our and another's subjectivity. I release in order that I may be in awe and at awe as I behold—not merely recognize—the truth of my life and your life and other's lives. The Jesuit Anthony de Mello writes, "It is only inasmuch as you see someone as he or she really is here and now and not as they are in your memory or your desire or in your imagination or projection that you can truly love them, otherwise it is not the person that you love but the idea that you have formed of this person, or this person as the object of your desire not as he or she is in themselves."[2] We will never become,

2. Mello, The Way to Love, 97.

or make space for others to become, what we, and they, most desire until we release our clinging. We are made to be subjects who desire, not objects of desire. We are made to be subjects who seek a God who asserts that all captives are now set free. This is a theological basis for recognition, and for that which we dare to hope to be known as: loved, loveable, and loving.

In this last chapter, I offer a meditation on a self-in-relation constituted by co-becoming. While this epilogue is primarily a self-reflexive meditation, it is grounded in the following claims:

1. I argue that those of us who teach and research from the location of feminist pastoral theology are invited to engage in an untaming process in giving accounts where the circuit of recognition-assertion is at work. An untaming is an invitation to participate in a life of sacred wilderness. In participating in a life of sacred wilderness, we make possible our ability to give and receive accounts of selves that can be held in love, even imperfectly and while acknowledging optimal failure.

2. Acknowledging the sacred wilderness of all lives is a theological practice that gives rise to self and communal blessing. To agree to practice recognition of the wild, that is, to be led into relational unknowns without desiring to fix or stabilize an other self, is the means by which we are optimally constituted in our co-becoming. It is important to note that co-becoming, like the circuits of recognition-assertion explored vis a vis Benjamin, Butler, and Althaus-Reid, is a fine circuit. Wires can easily be crossed and still we function, though not always optimally. Co-becoming may slip into manipulation or domination-submission. However, it is by co-becoming's intentional and deliberate practice of self and communal blessing that these which lead to domination or submission, and not co-becoming, may be recircuited.

3. Lastly, co-becoming is a deep spirituality of complex subjectivity and relationality in the midst of suffering and social injustice. This spirituality beckons us toward postures of receptive action through which we may encounter the loveliness of another subject. These encounters are opportunities for mutual beholding. Postures of beholding create the space for grace—not merely a feeling or intuitive sense of gift, but a spatially and temporally oriented thing that saturates existence—to be recognized, revealed, and unveiled.

Teleologically, this orientation acknowledges multiple ends, some of which may rub hard and grate against each other. And again, the process of co-becoming further elicits the constitution of selves-in-relation as an open horizon of knowing and being known as loved, loveable, and loving.

A feminist pastoral theology of a self-in-relation constituted by co-becoming is a deep spirituality. While spiritualities are located within religious traditions, they also arise from engagement with the vicissitudes and joys of living. This spirituality of recognition arises from the tension of living in the sea in between complete assertion and complete recognition. In actuality, complete and completed assertion and recognition are not helpful practices. When we think that we have completed the circuit, closed the loop of recognition and assertion, we have ceased our growth into and through a complex spirituality of becoming. As such, this feminist pastoral theology of a self-in-relation constituted by co-becoming forfeits tidy definition and closure while consciously and intentionally saying yes to an open horizon.

## Like a Wild Woman

In previous chapters I argued that subjects may be recognized, misrecognized, or not recognized at all. When circuits of recognition go awry and subjects are misrecognized or not recognized, feminist pastoral theology must actively name the constraints that impede the ability to hear marginalized voices. We act in solidarity in order to enable hearing, as well as telling. By using the word telling, I mean to imply that our pastoral theological accounts of subjectivity must be undertaken with a goal of empowering marginalized voices to tell their own stories. Telling and hearing may be construed to imply a hyper-rational, masculinized discourse defined by features which make little or no space for the affective, embodied dimensions of life. However, as has been the contention of this study, this is precisely the kind of telling and hearing that is incomplete and which contributes to ongoing patterns of misrecognition and non-recognition. While pastoral theology as a whole has paid particular attention to the ground of human experience, I would like to suggest that practicing giving untamed accounts in feminist pastoral theology is a response to an incomplete, though never complete, telling and hearing.

Without space to hear or to tell untamed accounts, the shackles of domination and submission become not only possible, but attractive.

To delve into the heart of women's experience is to return to a landscape of wilderness. The wilderness of experience is a place of fertility, as well as potential dangers to those who are not familiar with the terrain: women's bodies, emotions, relations, and vocations. These dark and dangerous places which must formerly be tamed and exposed, are now claimed as central and necessary to the advancement of caring and justice-making from pastoral theological standpoints. What does it mean to give untamed accounts in feminist pastoral theology? What does it mean to see the sacred wilderness in another? To take up these questions, we must first ask what the wilderness holds and then describe how seeing our life through this framework is liberatory.

It is rare for me not to take a daily walk in the woods, and although this is not an expansive wilderness, a mere hundred acres, I often find myself running along deer trails, crawling under and over downed limbs, and frequently disoriented as I follow my beagle dog Ruby as she does what comes instinctually: hunt and give chase. She goes off the path, leading me deeper into less familiar places. Often I lose track of her and must simply trust that she will find me again. There is an unknown quality in these woods, particularly when I walk at the edge of dusk. The darkness descends and, with practice, I continue to learn how to walk in the dark, both slowly and fast, trusting that I will find the right footing, even when it leads me off the established path. I tramp along other ways that are now revealed, learning to love walking in the dark.

"There are paths that can be followed, and there is a path that cannot—it is not a path, it is the wilderness," writes Pulitzer Prize-winning poet Gary Snyder.[3] Giving an account of oneself and creating the conditions for other selves to give their accounts necessitates a willingness to hear multiple and, perhaps, conflicting accounts of subjectivity that may lead off-path. Going off the path of neatly marked out subjectivities and identities is also the way of the wild. Going off the path does not mean abandoning one's upbringing, one's identities, one's unconsciously learned mode of being in the world; these are pieces of the self that cannot be abandoned. They are deep formations. Going into the wild is an invitation to examine these formations, as much as we are able to see them.

3. Snyder, "On the Path, Off the Trail," 162.

Despite all the deep knowledge and practice of queering gender, I am still schooled in my femininity. By walking, tramping, and giving chase in the woods, I am invited to confront fears that I have about what I am allowed or expected to do. My one hundred acres are a good place to practice stepping into the unknown. Doing so, I deschool my self-in-relation who has been taught that the wild is a chaotic, unordered space, no place for someone like me. On the contrary, I have learned that the wild is a fertile place, a good and holy place. It is a fruitful place for those willing to learn through observation and engagement. Still, the wild is also a dangerous place. Acknowledging this danger—that I may take a hard fall and hurt myself, that I may wander or get lost, that I may encounter animals or humans and take them by surprise—elicits an acknowledgment that all of our lives are filled with danger. This danger is both by our own making and unmaking, and also through no particular actions that we have taken or desire to take. We cannot get away from danger, despite alarming calls to do so from internal and external voices.

Despite alarms of potential danger, the practice of the wild is ultimately a call to embrace freedom, which is, in itself, dangerous. To recognize another is to recognize their wilderness, their undomestication, and their untamedness (or at least the potential for all these things). The call to be careful (and care filled) honors and respects the other who is both wounded and powerful. This recognition of wounds and power creates the conditions by which we might approach another: with gentle strength; with curiosity at another's experience and becoming in the wilds of the world; and with a willingness to engage on another's terms, following them into the wild until we must leave that path, and choosing or being chosen by another path.

Embracing the wilderness as part of a feminist pastoral theological project of recognition is vital to living into the tension of optimal recognition and assertion. Optimal recognition is ultimately about learning to love differently: in freedom, in openness, acknowledging the danger that we cannot escape because we live our lives in a horizon of care in which we are failed and in which we also fail others, especially those we care about. Failures in recognizing and asserting may be failures in care, but they are not irreparable. Standing in the wild places invites us to go down trails where our hearts become untamed. Untaming our hearts, removing the tightly wound barbwire which constricts the pulse of sacred life, makes possible the hearing of another's story and responding honorably, perceiving those things left unsaid but which we may begin to perceive, even incompletely and imperfectly, as fellow untamed, unruly, undomesticated, yet still fragile, pilgrims.

## Self and Communal Blessings in the Midst of the Unknown

When we agree to see what we already are—women and men of the wild—opportunities unfold in our becoming. Creatures of the wild are both strong and wounded. We are this way often as a result of events beyond our control, events of birth and deep psychosocial formation. Injuries to the self-in-relation, no matter their origin, are woven into the texture of our lives. Injustice and suffering are woven into the texture of our lives. Yet, in our wilderness (and from the wilderness) we petition the other to recognize our becoming, even as we bravely undergo a set of transformations which make evident the instability and unfixed nature of our subjectivity. A self-in-relation emerges in the present even as the future unknown unfolds. Despite unknowing, we may choose self and communal blessing. We may practice with deep theological convictions anchoring us to bless the others within ourselves and others outside ourselves as we and they journey on and off the trail of becoming. These are the blessings of co-becoming, allowing a self to be unveiled without making them through force or manipulation.

I invite dear ones with me to my hikes. They give answers of yes, no, and maybe in accompanying me along the journey. Still, I hike. I know that I choose difficult terrain in my hikes alone, and I often forget when I invite others that the landscape may be too difficult, our paces too different. Though I too have sustained injuries, as most have, my daily hikes are a commitment to strengthen the underlying muscle. Still, as we hike together – these friends and family, all of whom I see as loveable, valuable, and honorable—I know that I cannot attend fully to their wounds, wrought by the vicissitudes of existence. I recognize their pain. I choose to slow my pace, to stretch, to linger in a spot as we both catch our breath. I tell a story or two. I point out some curvature of a piece of wood that pleases me. I note the sun's position and turn myself 360° to see how the light plays amongst the trail, off the path, and deep into the woods. We pause and discuss what we each desire, where our energy lies, and how much is available for this project we have embarked upon. When both our energies are depleted, we find ourselves in agreement: "Let us go, and be returned. Let us go home," we say.

Yet, when I desire to press on, or the Other desires to press on, our discernment for life together must necessarily take a turn. We have come together and so we face the challenge of leaving each other. "I will find another way home," I say. However, I know that if I wander too long, pick up another trail, or become disoriented in my travails, I may find another home, another path, another room in the spiritual mansion, which may not be for my friend what it is for me. Which cannot be for my friend what it is for me. Sometimes I find myself saying, "I am going deeper into the wilderness and I must go alone." The Other says, "Don't do that." She cajoles, "Just come with me." "I cannot," I say. She can choose to accept what my becoming makes of me, and what it makes of us, or not. Still, I must go. The French philosopher Luce Irigaray writes, "To accept not to make, in favor of a letting be, is a gesture required for turning back to the ground of oneself and for recognizing the other as other."[4]

When she recognizes me as other, an optimal recognition which must necessarily include failure, our being and becoming unfolds across the horizon of living with and caring about each other. We tenderly care for each other. We hold each other, our hearts aligned, our heads cradled in the hollows of each others' shoulders. We know all too well the fragility of our choosing. In acknowledging this fragility, we both recognize and assert the making of our agential subjectivity. Our very selves are made and remade in this moment (and in every moment). We are constituted and reconstituted as our words and gestures beckon forth who we become in gestures of blessing.

I know that I am held, loved, and blessed in this relationship. Unlike the patriarch Jacob who wrestled with God, I did not need to wrestle with my friend to receive my blessing. Nor was I struck down, like the apostle Paul. Forceful actions which may cause physical, psychic, or spiritual harm do not befall me through her hand. I know that this is not always the case for so many other selves-in-relation who venture forth in their becoming. My friend has come to understand that the project of my becoming is mine, through relationship with Divinity, to call into existence, and she is willing to release me. She understands that the project of my becoming is mine to make, even while acknowledging social constraints. She cannot go to the wilderness for me. Irigaray reminds us, "The other

---

4. Irigaray, *The Way of Love*, 123.

cannot serve as a resource for our project, our action. In the constitution of a human horizon, the other must remain an other, someone different with whom to learn how to live together and to dialogue."[5] She liberates me; she does not fix me.

Yet, this project of becoming was never mine alone. She has become part of my becoming, and I, hers. We are co-becoming. Our co-becoming is made possible by our willingness to release each other. We agree to assert ourselves and to recognize each other in ways that actively resist the project of domination and submission. We both unfold and unveil in front of each other as we consciously and intentionally choose each other's presence, acknowledging our vulnerability and wounds as well as our strengths and courage. We acknowledge the uniqueness of each other. Our uniqueness is always unfolding, based on our wounds and healed places. I know that I may not perceive her correctly, and I ask her to show me where I have misunderstood. Our misunderstandings are relational. In our co-becoming, we agree to be open to apprehending each other in the incomplete fullness of our being. Again, we know full well that failure is guaranteed. I continue to be, potentially, subject to manipulation, to violence, to indescribable pain as a subject constituted by co-becoming. Yet, we persist in our intentions of honoring and loving through recognition.

Because we speak of things on the spiritual plane, I give my consent to her to bless me. She also gives me her consent to receive my blessing. What we choose to do is bless, without force. Our giving of a blessing is a claim of relationality. We find ourselves moving into receptive postures, perceiving each other and ourselves as best as we can as we awaken to the vicissitudes and joys that make and unmake our becoming.

When we give accounts of ourselves to each other, we know that we might be recognized, misrecognized, or not recognized at all. I do not give my consent to misrecognition or non-recognition, but I acknowledge that even our care-filled intersubjective exchanges of blessing, performed in hope and joy, may miss the mark. The instability of my identity which draws me toward transformation may also cause misrecognition or non-recognition. Still, we practice grace as we recognize that personal transformations make way for social transformations. We offer grace in order to make space for relational redress as a movement toward justice. As the same time, our willingness to receive relational redress when

5. Ibid., 116.

misrecognized or not recognized may or may not be possible given our capacity to grapple with the unknown qualities of each other's subjectivity. Unfolding and unveiling are not always pleasant.

Sometimes, foreclosure in our project of co-becoming occurs. The accounts that have arisen from doing life together may come into such conflict with our perception of the other that, for the sake of justice, I may have to take my leave, or she, hers. Otherwise, my blessing may morph into curse, my love become shackles. Shackles, as Jessica Benjamin suggests, need not be permanent in our relationships with each other. We need not continue to act out our pathogenic belief cycles, our deepest anxieties, and fears about our loveability as selves-in-relation constituted by co-becoming. Nor must we be subject to an Other's pathogenic belief cycles, our deepest anxieties, or fears. We may courageously live into a spiritual practice of mutual beholding.

## A Spirituality of Mutual Beholding

"Behold the Lamb of God who takes away the sin of the world," intones Fr. Gene at the apex of the Eucharistic liturgy, a man I first met over ten years ago while a Master's student in theology. Whether I choose to call this encounter serendipitous or divinely orchestrated, the machinations of my life have once again brought me into his presence. A happy coincidence made possible by an encounter with a Nashville acquaintance turned Cincinnatian who mentioned the church she was attending and the priest's name. It is a return I longed for without knowing.

The first time I showed up for worship at St. Francis de Sales Parish, a namesake which is full of remembrances and meaning having been educated by Oblates of St. Francis de Sales through my high school and undergraduate institution, I relish in watching surprise register across Fr. Gene's face as he greets folks in the pew. He recognizes me. I watch him apprehend me in my difference; his mouth opens. Who I once was when I cantored and led music over a decade ago is different. I look different. I am different. I am no longer who I once was. Yet, I am recognized. I am seen. I am beheld in light of my transformations.

I remember the becoming that I petitioned those ten plus years ago. My journals from that time reflect the things that I wanted to achieve and become, degrees and experiences that are now realized, though not all and with many moments of foreclosure. It is difficult to describe exactly this uncanny moment. I am home, but not. All is familiar, and not famil-iar at all. This uncanny moment breaks open and I remember the present. The gifts that I have received along the journey thus far become more ful-ly integrated in my co-becoming. I experience this laugh-cry existence, this wild woman existence, as I live the past in the present differently. I recognize this liturgy, this work of the people. I give my yes to a becoming in which I do not fully know yet what it means, how it will undo what I have constructed in my world, what it will mean to be known again in this place of grace.

What does it mean for me to enter, again, into this place of grace, which also may be a place of constriction? The gothic architecture and stain glass windows tell me stories about the history of Christianity, a place that from the exterior (and sometimes from the interior) appears to be inhospitable to the constructed, but still real, Other. Will Sarah be recognized here? Will I be recognized here? Will Marcella Althaus-Reid's words on liberation theology and sexuality find a soft space in the hearts of believers who gather here? Will I speak of being undone by past rela-tionships that may not live up to a set of ecclesial-social norms, Judith Butler echoing in my head and heart? Does anyone else potentially per-ceive a pathogenic belief cycle that shackles when we say, "Lord, I am not worthy that you should enter under my roof, but only say the word and my soul shall be healed," before breaking bread with each other? The line between humility and humiliation, like subjectivity and subjectivation, is razor thin.

I participate in this institution and assert myself. On some days, I recognize my need for humility and intone with the faithful what we have learned to say. On other days, I remain silent and say in my heart, "I am and I am becoming worthy and healed through this relationship." I consider this my petitioning, not to Fr. Gene or to one of the ecclesial bodies through which I have come to understand the Christian tradition, but to a Creating God who is also co-becoming. Fr. Gene responds to us all, "May we become what we receive," and I recognize my vulnerability as well as Creating God's vulnerability as this God welcomes our partici-pation in the kin-dom. I ask that this Creating God behold me, and I, in turn, also agree to behold. I choose to practice this act of beholding not only in liturgical spaces, but in places where I encounter others both like me and not like me. In turn, I am also beheld.

As we behold each other, we acknowledge that we are different. In acknowledging difference, I have not consumed the Other, subjugated or fused, manipulated or coerced. Instead, we begin to mirror each other's goodness. We gaze in admiration and delight, not fixing, but attending with joy as we practice love that flowers in freedom and openness. Joy is reflected at seeing the other. Benedict of Nursia, famed for his monastic rule, tells us to open our eyes and see the *Deificum lumen*—"the light that makes the beholder divine."[6] In mutual beholding, we see the light of creation play over each other's features. Eye meets eye, and heart speaks to heart. We call each other beloved. We are kindred, receiving each other in grace and love, opening to the sacredness of each other. I am cared for justly as I am recognized.

Although I alone cannot change all the systems which sustain violence, misrecognition, and non-recognition, my opening to the sacredness of another allows me to strive for solidarity and justice with others. Still, I know that my knowledge of the Other is incomplete and will always be so. This space of unknowing begs for reverence. Silence falls on us. We cultivate both reverence and silence so that we might learn to love differently. Our carefully constructed and practiced self-narratives are no longer sufficient. We are all those narratives and also more than any telling could ever reveal. In our silence, we show ourselves. The wellsprings of life and death, birth and destruction, teem in our beholding. *Exitus et reditus*, exiting and returning. Uniquely each our own, we become ourselves again.

6. Steindl-Rast, *A Listening Heart*, 44.

# Bibliography

Abbey, Edward. *Desert Solitaire: A Season in the Wilderness*. New York: Ballantine, 1968.

Abernathey, Marti. "Memorializing 2013." http://tdor.info/memorializing-2013/.

Ackerly, Brooke A. *Political Theory and Feminist Social Criticism*. Contemporary Political Theory. Cambridge: Cambridge University Press, 2000.

Ackermann, Denise M. "'A Voice Was Heard in Ramah': A Feminist Theology of Praxis for Healing in South Africa." In *Liberating Faith Practices: Feminist Practical Theologies in Context*, edited by Denise M. Ackermann and Riet Bons-Storm, 75–102. Leuven: Peeters, 1998.

Adams, Carol J. *Woman-Battering*. Creative Pastoral Care and Counseling Series. Minneapolis: Fortress, 1994.

Ali, Carroll A. Watkins. *Survival and Liberation: Pastoral Theology in African American Context*. St. Louis: Chalice, 1999.

Althaus-Reid, Marcella. *From Feminist Theology to Indecent Theology: Readings on Poverty, Sexual Identity, and God*. London: SCM, 2004.

———. "Feetishism: The Scent of a Latin American Body Theology." In *Toward a Theology of Eros: Transfiguring Passion at the Limits of Discipline*, edited by Virginia Burrus and Catherine Keller, 134–52. New York: Fordham University Press, 2006.

———. "On Non-Docility and Indecent Theologians: A Response to the Panel for *Indecent Theology*." *Feminist Theology* 11 (January 2003), 182–89.

———. *The Queer God*. New York: Routledge, 2003.

———. "The Trouble with Normality." In *Latin American Liberation Theology: The Next Generation*, edited by Ivan Petrella, 42–68. Maryknoll, NY: Orbis, 2005.

Armour, Ellen T. and Susan M. St. Ville. "Judith Butler in Theory." In *Bodily Citations: Religion and Judith Butler*, edited by Ellen T. Armour and Susan M. St. Ville, 1–12. New York: Columbia University Press, 2006.

Baker-Fletcher, Karen. "The Erotic in Contemporary Black Women's Writings." In *Loving the Body: Black Religious Studies and the Erotic*, edited by Anthony B. Pinn and Dwight N. Hopkins, 199–213. New York: Palgrave, 2004.

Beekman, Daniel. "Hip-hop Won't Stop in the South Bronx at the Rebel Diaz Arts Collective." *New York Daily News*. March 3, 2011. http://articles.nydailynews.com/2011–03–03/local/28669521_1_hip-hop-immigration-law-factory/.

Benjamin, Jessica. *The Bonds of Love*. New York: Pantheon, 1988.

———. *Shadow of the Other: Intersubjectivity and Gender in Psychoanalysis*. New York: Routledge, 1997.

———. *Like Subjects, Love Objects: Essays on Recognition and Sexual Difference*. New Haven: Yale University Press, 1998.

Blain-Wallace, William. "The Politics of Tears: Lamentation as Justice-Making." In *Injustice and the Care of Souls*, edited by Sheryl A. Kujawa-Holbrook and Karen B. Montagno, 183–97. Minneapolis: Fortress, 2009.

Boisen, Anton. *Exploration of the Inner World*. New York: Willet, Clark, 1936.

Bourdieu, Pierre. *Outline of a Theory of Practice*. Translated by Richard Nice. Cambridge Studies in Social Anthropology 16. Cambridge: Cambridge University Press, 1977.

———. "Site Effects." In *Weight of the World: Social Suffering in Contemporary Society*. Translated by Priscilla Parkhurst Ferguson, Susan Emanuel, Joe Johnson, and Shoggy T. Waryn, 123–129. Stanford: Stanford University Press, 1999.

Breen, Margaret Soenser, and Warren J. Blumenfeld, with Susanna Baer, Robert Alana Brookey, Lynda Hall, Vicky Kirby, Diane Helene Miller, Robert Shail, and Natalie Wilson. "'There Is a Person Here': An Interview with Judith Butler." *International Journal of Sexuality and Gender Studies* 6/1–2 (2001) 7–23.

Brookey, Robert Alan, and Diane Helene Miller. "Changing Signs: The Political Pragmatism of Poststructuralism." *International Journal of Sexuality and Gender Studies* 6/1–2 (2001) 139–53.

Browning, Don S. *A Fundamental Practical Theology: Descriptive and Strategic Proposals*. Minneapolis: Fortress, 1996.

———. "The Past and Possible Future of Religion and Psychological Studies." In *Religion and Psychology: Mapping the Terrain*, edited by Diane Jonte-Pace and William B. Parsons, 165–80. New York: Routledge, 2001.

———. *Religious Ethics and Pastoral Care*. Theology and Pastoral Care Series. Philadelphia: Fortress, 1983.

Brubaker, Rogers, and Frederick Cooper. "Beyond 'Identity.'" *Theory and Society* 29 (2000) 1–47.

Butler, Judith. *Bodies That Matter: On the Discursive Limits of "Sex."* New York: Routledge, 1993.

———. *Gender Trouble: Feminism and the Subversion of Identity*. 2nd ed. New York: Routledge, 1999.

———. *Giving an Account of Oneself*. New York: Fordham University Press, 2005.

———. *Precarious Life: The Powers of Mourning and Violence*. New York: Verso, 2004.

———. *The Psychic Life of Power: Theories in Subjection*. Stanford: Stanford University Press, 1997.

Certeau, Michel de. *The Practice of Everyday Life*. Translated by Steven Rendall. Berkeley: University of California Press, 1984.

Chodorow, Nancy J. *The Reproduction of Mothering: Psychoanalysis and the Sociology of Gender*. 2nd ed. Berkeley: University of California Press, 1999.

Clebsch, William A., and Charles R. Jaeckle. *Pastoral Care in Historical Perspective*. New York: Harper, 1967.

Clinebell, Howard. *Basic Types of Pastoral Care and Counseling*. Nashville: Abingdon, 1984.

Collins, Patricia Hill. *Black Feminist Thought: Knowledge, Consciousness, and the Politics of Empowerment*. New York: Routledge, 2008.

Connolly, William E. *Identity\Difference: Democratic Negotiations of Political Paradox*. Minneapolis: University of Minnesota Press, 1991.

Cooper-White, Pamela. "Com|plicated Woman." In *Braided Selves: Collected Essays on Multiplicity, God, and Persons*, 135–155. Eugene, OR: Cascade Books, 2011.

———. *Cry of Tamar: Violence against Women and the Church's Response*. Minneapolis: Fortress, 1995.

———. *Many Voices: Pastoral Psychotherapy in Relational and Theological Perspective*. Minneapolis: Fortress, 2007.

Cravioto, Alejando, et al. *Final Report of the Independent Panel of Experts on the Cholera Outbreak in Haiti*. New York: United Nations, 2011. http://www.un.org/news/dh/infocus/haiti/un-cholera-report-final.pdf/.

Crenshaw, Kimberlé Williams. "Mapping the Margins: Intersectionality, Identity Politics, and Violence against Women of Color." *Stanford Law Review* 43 (1991) 1241–99.

Davey D and Jenny on the Block. "NYC Police Beat Up Rap Group Members Rebel Diaz." *NYC Indymedia*. June 18, 2008. http://nyc.indymedia.org/en/2008/06/98039.html.

Delany, Samuel R. *Times Square Red, Times Square Blue*. New York: New York University Press, 1999.

Deveaux, Monique. "Shifting Paradigms: Theorizing Care and Justice in Political Theory." *Hypatia* 10 (Spring 1995) 115–19.

Doehring, Carrie. "A Method of Feminist Pastoral Theology." In *Feminist and Womanist Pastoral Theology*, edited by Bonnie J. Miller-McLemore and Brita L. Gill-Austern, 95–111. Nashville: Abingdon, 1999.

Douglas, Kelly Brown. "The Black Church and the Politics of Sexuality." In *Loving the Black Body: Black Religious Studies and the Erotic*, edited by Anthony B. Pinn and Dwight Hopkins, 347–362. New York: Palgrave, 2004.

Dunlap, Susan. *Counseling Depressed Women*. Louisville: Westminster John Knox, 1997.

Erzen, Tanya. *Straight to Jesus: Sexual and Christian Conversion in the Ex-Gay Movement*. Berkeley: University of California Press, 2006.

Fanon, Frantz. *Black Skin, White Masks*. Translated by Richard Philcox. With a foreword by Kwame Anthony Appiah. New York: Grove, 2008.

Farmer, Paul. "On Suffering and Structural Violence: A View from Below." In *Social Suffering*, edited by Arthur Kleinman, Veena Das, and Margaret Lock, 261–84. Berkeley: University of California Press, 1997.

Fisher, Nigel. "Haiti: 6 Months After . . ." New York: United Nations, 2010. http://www.un.org/en/peacekeeping/missions/minustah/documents/6_months_after_commemoration.pdf/.

Fraser, James C. "The Relevance of Human Geography for Studying Urban Disasters." *Space and Culture* 9 (Feb. 2006) 14–19.

Fraser, Nancy. *Scales of Justice: Reimagining Political Space in a Globalizing World*. New York: Columbia University Press, 2009.

Fraser, Nancy, and Axel Honneth. *Redistribution or Recognition?: A Political-Philosophical Exchange*. New York: Verso, 2003.

Froehle, Mary, et al. "Complex Identities in Ministry Formation: Processes of Reflection, Refraction, and Diffraction in the Context of Difference in Theological Field Education." In *Complex Identities in a Shifting World: Practical Theological Perspectives*, edited by Pamela Couture, et al., 19–30. International Journal of Practical Theology 17. Zurich: Lit, 2015.

Gill-Austern, Brita L. "Engaging Diversity and Difference: From Practices of Exclusion to Practices of Practical Solidarity." In *Injustice and the Care of Souls*, edited by Sheryl A. Kujawa-Holbrook and Karen B. Montagno, 29–44. Minneapolis: Fortress, 2009.

Gómez, Luis A. "Evo Morales Turns the Tide of History." In *Dispatches from Latin America: On the Frontlines Against Neoliberalism*, edited by Teo Ballvé and Vijay Prashed, 140–47. Cambridge, MA: South End, 2006.

Graham, Elaine L. *Making the Difference: Gender, Personhood, and Theology*. Minneapolis: Fortress, 1996.

———. *Representations of the Post/Human: Monsters, Aliens, and Others in Popular Culture*. New Brunswick, NJ: Rutgers University Press, 2002.

———. Review of *Representations of the Post/Human: Monsters, Aliens, and Others in Popular Culture*, by Clive Marsh. *Political Theology* 5 (2004) 123–25.

———. *Transforming Practice: Pastoral Theology in an Age of Uncertainty*. 1996. Reprinted, Eugene, OR: Wipf & Stock, 1996.

Greider, Kathleen J. "'Too Militant?' Aggression, Gender, and the Construction of Justice." In *Through the Eyes of Women: Insights for Pastoral Care*, edited by Jeanne Stevenson Moessner, 123–42. Minneapolis: Fortress, 1996.

Gross, Michael Joseph. "The grass is very dark to be from the white heads of old mothers." In *Open House: Writers Redefine Home*, edited by Mark Doty, 145–60. St. Paul: Graywolf, 2003.

Grosskurth, Phyllis. "The New Psychology of Women." *New York Review of Books*, October 24, 1991, 25–32.

Harré Rom, and W. Gerrod Parrott, eds. *The Emotions: Social, Cultural, and Biological Dimensions*. Thousand Oaks, CA: Sage, 1996.

Held, Virginia. "The Meshing of Care and Justice." *Hypatia* 10 (Spring 1995) 128–32.

Hiltner, Seward. *Preface to Pastoral Theology*. New York: Abingdon, 1958.

Hutchins, Christina K. "Unconforming Becomings: The Significance of Whitehead's Novelty and Butler's Subversion for the Repetitions of Lesbian Identity and the Expansion of the Future." In *Bodily Citations: Religion and Judith Butler*, edited by Ellen T. Armour and Susan M. St. Ville, 120–56. New York: Columbia University Press, 2006.

Illich, Ivan. *Medical Nemesis: The Expropriation of Health*. New York: Pantheon, 1982.

Irigaray, Luce. *The Way of Love*. Translated by Heidi Bostick and Stephen Pluhácek. NewYork: Continuum, 2002.

Isasi-Díaz, Ada María. *En la Lucha/In the Struggle: A Hispanic Women's Liberation Theology*. Minneapolis: Fortress, 1993.

Johnson, Cedric C. "Resistance Is not Futile: Finding Therapeutic Space between Colonialism and Globalization." In *Healing Wisdom: Depth Psychology and the Pastoral Ministry*, edited by Kathleen J. Greider, Deborah van Deusen Hunsinger, and Felicity Brock Kelcourse, 157–75. Grand Rapids: Eerdmans, 2010.

King, Robert. "Death and Resurrection of an Urban Church." *Faith and Leadership*. March 24, 2015. https://www.faithandleadership.com/death-and-resurrection-urban-church.

Kittay, Eva Feder. "The Personal Is Philosophical Is Political: A Philosopher and Mother of a Cognitively Disabled Person Sends Notes from the Battlefield." In *Cognitive Disability and Its Challenge to Moral Philosophy*, edited by Eva Feder Kittay and

Licia Carlson, 393–413. Metaphilosophy Series in Philosophy. Malden, MA: Wiley-Blackwell, 2010.

Kornfeld, Margaret. *Cultivating Wholeness: A Guide to Care and Counseling in Faith Communities*. New York: Continuum, 2008.

Kujawa-Holbrook, Sheryl, and Karen B. Montagno, eds. *Injustice and the Care of Souls: Taking Oppression Seriously in Pastoral Care*. Minneapolis: Fortress, 2009.

Larsen, Nella. *Passing: Authoritative Text, Backgrounds and Contexts, Criticism*. Edited by Carla Kaplan. Norton Critical Edition. New York: Norton, 2007.

Lartey, Emmanuel. *In Living Color: An Intercultural Approach to Pastoral Care and Counseling*. 2nd ed. Philadelphia: Kingsley, 2003.

Lassiter, Kate. "No Easy Resolution: Feminist Pastoral Theology and the Challenge of Identity." *Journal of Pastoral Theology* 23 (July 2013) 4.1–4.12.

Mahler, Margaret, et al. *The Psychological Birth of the Human Infant: Symbiosis and Individuation*. New York: Basic, 1975.

Marshall, Joretta L. *Counseling Lesbian Partners*. With a foreword by Andrew Lester. Louisville: Westminster John Knox, 1997.

———. "Models of Understanding Differences, Dialogues, and Discourses: From Sexuality to Queer Theory in Learning and Teaching Care." *Journal of Pastoral Theology* 19 (2009) 29–47.

———. Review of *Counseling Lesbian Partners*, by James I. Higginbotham. *Encounters* 60 (1999) 109–11.

———. Review of *Counseling Lesbian Partners*, by Nancy J. Ramsay. *Journal of Pastoral Theology* 7 (1997) 166–68.

Martín-Baró, Ignacio. *Writings for a Liberation Psychology*. Edited by Adrianne Aron and Shawn Corne. Translated by Adrianne Aron. Cambridge: Harvard University Press, 1996.

McClure, Barbara J. *Moving beyond Individualism in Pastoral Care and Counseling: Reflections on Theory, Theology, and Practice*. Eugene, OR: Cascade Books, 2010.

McGarrah Sharp, Melinda A. *Misunderstanding Stories: Toward a Postcolonial Pastoral Theology*. Eugene, OR: Pickwick Publications, 2013.

McKnight, John L. *The Careless Society: Community and Its Counterfeits*. New York: Basic Books, 1996.

Mello, Anthony de. *The Way to Love: The Last Meditations of Anthony de Mello*. New York: Doubleday, 1991.

Miller-McLemore, Bonnie J. "Cognitive Science and the Question of Theological Method." *Journal of Pastoral Theology* 20 (2010) 67–78.

———. "Feminist Theory in Pastoral Theology." In *Feminist and Womanist Pastoral Theology*, edited by Bonnie J. Miller-McLemore and Brita L. Gill-Austern, 77–94. Nashville: Abingdon, 1999.

———. "The Living Human Web: Pastoral Theology at the Turn of the Century." In *Through the Eyes of Women: Insights for Pastoral Care*, edited by Jeanne Stevenson Moessner, 9–26. Minneapolis: Fortress, 1996.

———. "Pastoral Theology as Public Theology: Revolutions in the 'Fourth Area.'" In *Pastoral Care and Counseling: Redefining the Paradigms*, edited by Nancy J. Ramsay, 45–64. Nashville: Abingdon, 2004.

———. "Practical Theology and Pedagogy: Embodying Theological Know-How." In *For Life Abundant: Practical Theology, Theological Education, and Christian*

*Ministry*, edited by Dorothy C. Bass and Craig Dykstra, 170–90. Grand Rapids: Eerdmans, 2008.

———. "The Subject and Practice of Pastoral Theology: Pushing Past the Nagging Identity Crisis to the Poetics of Resistance." In *Liberating Faith Practices: Feminist Practical Theologies in Context*, edited by Denise M. Ackermann and Riet Bons-Storm, 175–98. Leuven: Peeters, 1998.

Miller-McLemore, Bonnie J., and Brita L. Gill-Austern, eds. "Introduction." In *Feminist and Womanist Pastoral Theology*, 13–20. Nashville: Abingdon, 1999.

Mogel, Lize, and Alexis Bhagat, eds. *An Atlas of Radical Cartography*. Los Angeles: Journal of Aesthetics and Protest Press, 2008.

Neuger, Christie Cozad. "Power and Difference in Pastoral Theology." In *Pastoral Care and Counseling: Redefining the Paradigms*, edited by Nancy J. Ramsay, 65–85. Nashville: Abingdon, 2004.

Noor, Jaisal. "Judge Dismisses Case against Rebel Diaz, says 'Keep up the good work.'" *The Indypendent*. June 22, 2009. http://www.indypendent.org/2009/06/22/ rebeldiazfree/.

Nussbaum, Martha. "Justice." In *Examined Life: Excursions with Contemporary Thinkers*, edited by Astra Taylor, 115–32. New York: New Press, 2009.

———. "The Professor of Parody." *The New Republic*. February 22, 1999. http://www. tnr.com/archive/0299/022299/nussbaum022299.html/.

Oatley, Keith, et al. *Understanding Emotions*. 2nd ed. Malden, MA: Wiley-Blackwell, 2006.

Oliver, Kelly. *Witnessing: Beyond Recognition*. Minneapolis: University of Minnesota Press, 2001.

Ortner, Sherry B. *Making Gender: The Politics and Erotics of Culture*. Boston: Beacon, 1996.

Parsons, Susan F. "The Boundaries of Desire: A Consideration of Judith Butler and Carter Heyward." *Feminist Theology* 8 (2008) 90–104.

Person, Ethel Spector. "Why It's So Sweet to Surrender." *New York Times*, February 26, 1989.

Polaris, "Sex Trafficking in the U.S." http://www.polarisproject.org/human-trafficking/ sex-trafficking-in-the-us/.

Pui-Lan, Kwok. "Body and Pleasure in Postcoloniality." In *Dancing Theology in Fetish Boots: Essays in Honour of Marcella Althaus-Reid*, edited by Lisa Isherwood and Mark D. Jordan, 31–43. London: SCM, 2010.

———. "Theology as a Sexual Act." *Feminist Theology* 11 (2003) 149–56.

Ramsay, Nancy J. "Contemporary Pastoral Theology: A Wider Vision for the Practice of Love." In *Pastoral Care and Counseling: Redefining the Paradigms*, edited by Nancy J. Ramsay, 155–76. Nashville: Abingdon, 2004.

Rans, Susan, and Mary H. Nelson. "Asset Based Community Development." 16 November 2011, Institute of Pastoral Studies, Loyola University Chicago, Chicago.

Réage, Pauline. *The Story of O*. Translated by Sabine d'Estreé. New York: Ballantine, 1965.

Rebel Diaz. "Guilty." *#Occupy the Airwaves*. 2011, MP3.

———. "Que'Sta Pasando! (Featuring Divine of the D.E.Y.)." *Otro Guerrillero Mixtape*, Vol. 2. 2008, compact disc.

———. "Which Side Are You On?" *Otro Guerillero Mixtape*, Vol. 2. 2008, compact disc.

Rivera, Mayra Rivera. "Corporeal Visions and Apparitions: The Narrative Strategies of an Indecent Theologian." In *Dancing Theology in Fetish Boots: Essays in Honour of Marcella Althaus-Reid*, edited by Lisa Isherwood and Mark D. Jordan, 79–94. London: SCM, 2010.

Rudy, Kathy. *Sex and the Church: Gender, Homosexuality, and the Transformation of Christian Ethics*. Boston: Beacon, 1997.

Salih, Sara, *Judith Butler*. New York: Routledge, 2002.

———. ed. *The Judith Butler Reader*. Malden, MA: Blackwell, 2004.

Sax, William S. *God Of Justice: Ritual Healing and Social Justice in the Central Himalayas*. New York: Oxford University Press, 2009.

Scheper-Hughes, Nancy. *Death without Weeping: The Violence of Everyday Life in Brazil*. Berkeley: University of California Press, 1992.

Schneider, Laurel C. *Beyond Monotheism: A Theology of Multiplicity*. New York: Routledge, 2008.

Schultz, Jim. "The Cochabamba Water Revolt and Its Aftermath." In *Dignity and Defiance: Stories from Bolivia's Challenge to Globalization*, edited by Jim Schultz and Melissa Crane Draper, 9–42. Berkeley: University of California, 2008.

Sen, Amartya. *Development as Freedom*. New York: Knopf, 1999.

Smith, Archie, Jr. *The Relational Self: Ethics and Therapy from a Black Church Perspective*. Nashville: Abingdon, 1982.

Snorton, Teresa. "The Legacy of the African American Matriarch." In *Through the Eyes of Women: Insights for Pastoral Care*, edited by Jeanne Stevenson Moessner, 50–65. Minneapolis: Fortress, 1996.

Snyder, Gary. *The Practice of the Wild*. Berkeley: Counterpoint, 1990.

Steindl-Rast, David. *A Listening Heart: The Spirituality of Sacred Sensuousness*. New York: Crossroads, 1999.

Susser, Ida, ed. *The Castells Reader on Cities and Social Theory*. Malden, MA: Blackwell, 2002.

Tillich, Paul. *Systematic Theology*. Vol. 1. Chicago: University of Chicago Press, 1951.

Townes, Emilie M. "Marcella Althaus-Reid's *Indecent Theology*: A Response." In *Dancing Theology in Fetish Boots: Essays in Honour of Marcella Althaus-Reid*, edited by Lisa Isherwood and Mark D. Jordan, 61–67. London: SCM, 2010.

Tracy, David. *Blessed Rage for Order: The New Pluralism In Theology*. 1975. Reprinted, Chicago: University of Chicago Press, 1996.

Wacquant, Loïc J. D. "America as Social Dystopia: The Politics of Urban Disintegration, or the French Uses of the 'American Model.'" In *The Weight of the World: Social Suffering in Contemporary Society*. Translated by Priscilla Parkhurst Ferguson, Susan Emanuel, Joe Johnson, and Shoggy T. Waryn, 130–39. Stanford: Stanford University Press, 1999.

Watson, Natalie K. "Unclosetting the Divine, or To the Midlands via Buenos Aires: Doing Sexual Theology after Marcella." In *Dancing Theology in Fetish Boots: Essays in Honour of Marcella Althaus-Reid*, edited by Lisa Isherwood and Mark D. Jordan, 191–199. London: SCM, 2010.

Winnicott, D. W. *Playing and Reality*. London: Tavistock, 1971.

Young, Iris Marion. *Justice and the Politics of Difference*. Princeton: Princeton University Press, 1990.

Žižek, Slavoj. *Violence: Six Sideways Reflections*. Big Ideas/Small Books. New York: Picador, 2008.

# Index